T0169441

Teacher You Are Enough & More

TEACHER
You Are Enough
& More

A Guide to Uplift Educators

CLAIRE RACHEL MAGHTAS
& KAREN JEAN EPPS

NASHVILLE

NEW YORK • LONDON • MELBOURNE • VANCOUVER

Teacher You Are Enough & More

A Guide to Uplift Educators

© 2018 Claire Rachel Maghtas & Karen Jean Epps

All rights reserved. No portion of this book may be reproduced, stored in a retrieval system, or transmitted in any form or by any means—electronic, mechanical, photocopy, recording, scanning, or other—except for brief quotations in critical reviews or articles, without the prior written permission of the publisher.

Published in New York, New York, by Morgan James Publishing. Morgan James is a trademark of Morgan James, LLC. www.MorganJamesPublishing.com

The Morgan James Speakers Group can bring authors to your live event. For more information or to book an event visit The Morgan James Speakers Group at www.TheMorganJamesSpeakersGroup.com.

ISBN 9781683508991 paperback
ISBN 9781683509004 eBook
Library of Congress Control Number: 2017918839

Cover Design & Interior Design by:
Christopher Kirk
www.GFSstudio.com

Holy Bible, New International Version, NIV Copyright 1973, 1978, 1984, 2011 by Biblica, Inc. Used by permission. All rights reserved worldwide.

"Scripture quotations are from the Holy Bible, English Standard Version (ESV), Permanent Text Edition (2016). Copyright 2001 by Crossway Bibles, a publishing ministry of Good News Publishers. Used by permission. All rights reserved."

Scripture quotations marked (NLT) are taken from the Holy Bible, New Living Translation, copyright 1996, 2004, 2007 by Tyndale House Foundation. Used by Permission of Tyndale House Publishers, Inc., Carol Stream, IL, 60188. All rights reserved.

"Scripture taken from the NEW AMERICAN STANDARD BIBLE, (NASB) Copyright 1960, 1962, 1963, 1968, 1971, 1972, 1973, 1975, 1977, 1995 by The Lockman Foundation, Used by permission."

World English Bible (WEB) by Public Domain. The name "World English Bible" is trademarked.

Bible References used at BibleGateway.com

This book is not a reflection of any school district, person, people, or school location. The experiences contained within are a reflection of the authors' experiences collectively over a fifty-year span.

In an effort to support local communities, raise awareness and funds, Morgan James Publishing donates a percentage of all book sales for the life of each book to Habitat for Humanity Peninsula and Greater Williamsburg.

Get involved today! Visit
www.MorganJamesBuilds.com

Endorsements

"The ultimate goal of life is the acquisition of wisdom: Aristotle said wisdom is the combination of knowledge and character. Both are important but what guarantees real success in life is character. It is a process that starts very early in life guided, or more important "modeled", by parents and teachers. Karen and Claire's book is a very significant contribution in this area. Children will acquire the knowledge and virtues to make them good pro-social individuals by experiential osmosis, i.e., picking the examples of grownups, rather than just by teachers dispensing «notions». This book is very practical; it gives teachers experiential tools to keep up their spirits, their vision, in function of their very challenging "ministry" with children, in this rapidly changing and conflictive world."

Dr. Miguel Novak,

Former faculty at Boston College and Pepperdine University, Malibu, CA Former Director of Campus Ministry at the University of the Pacific, Stockton, CA Lay missionary and adult religious educator in the US and 6 other countries.

"When I was a very new educator, I wish I had a book like this! As an adopted child of God, I am excited to have read a book geared to teachers and the use of scriptures to be of encouragement to teachers at all levels of growth in their faith and profession. The focus is upon the personal desires of the teacher, as it pertains to the work, for the success of their students. The main idea is becoming your dream teacher through key ideas like: compassion, dealing with struggles and living your values, are touched on in this book. Living in these values are crucial for teachers regardless of the view and have helped in my daily success. Ultimately, these are the keys that you must learn in order to break the desire to leave the profession of teaching in the first several years. Thank you for a good reading that includes some experiences and ideas rooted in both secular and scriptural world views, which the Christian educator must learn to grapple with and balance daily."

Kawika Berthelette,
Public School Music Teacher and Church Worship Leader

"This book is packed full of useful confirmations and gratitude statements that every teacher needs to have on their desk. These are great to use as anchors to elevate the spirit into positive energy preparing us to be good role models for our students."

Charlene McDonald,
Public School Preschool teacher

"The title is fabulous as often times teachers are made to feel they are not enough and more is required. This book tells teachers "they are enough and more!" It gives us permission to boost ourselves into higher consciousness."

Bill Delve,
General Education Public School Teacher

"The varied topics that are touched upon encourage me when I am struggling during my day. Reading and reflecting upon the verses help uplift my spirit. Every teacher needs this book to refer to and reflect on in times of challenges when in need of a little pick-me-up."

Lindsey Jack,
General Education Public School Teacher

"How appropriate for a teacher to read about knowledge being silver and wisdom as gold and claim them as a crown on their head! There is power in expressing blessings and grace on ourselves instead of expecting others to do it."

Janet Fernandez,
General Education Public School Teacher.

"It's a goldmine of answers, love, encouragement, and inspiration to live in peace and harmony. This book is written for all the seasons in our life. It has faith-filled confirmations to get us through the day."

Bobi Walter,
Special Education teacher.

"This encouraging book, written by two long time and respected public-school teachers, offers being patient and giving positive advice for changing behavior and getting powerful results with students."

Chris Coble,
Public School Teacher Librarian

"The tools and strategies in the back of the book were excellent and useful to relieve tension and stress of everyday pressures. It is necessary to take a few minutes, without feeling guilty, during our busy day to meditate and focus upon our body and mind so we can give our best to our students."

Jerome Martinez,
Public School Art Teacher

"The experiences in this book touched my heart and I can relate to the stories shared because they have also happened to me through my years of teaching. This reminds me, with all the hard work, teachers do make a difference in student's lives."

Stephanie Nikolaou,
Retired Public School Teacher

Dedication

For all the hard-working educators committed to serving and training students as productive members of society helping our country succeed.

Contents

Foreword

By Dr. Vicki Caruana, America's Teacher

Two accomplished teachers, Claire and Karen co-authored this book of encouragement to uplift teachers through their daily challenges in the education world. This book is a reminder to stay in the Word and trust the promises of God to elevate the spirit to a positive mindset. It contains invigorating and uplifting scripture to help educators maintain balance, peace and the renewal of the mind. They have also shared inspirational and personal stories teachers can relate to, similar to what I did in my book titled: *Apples & Chalkdust 180 Inspirational Stories and Encouragement for Teachers.*

One story from my book that comes to mind is when a former student saw his teacher by chance and recognized her. He proceeded to tell her he never forgot her as she was the only one who gave him a chance. After he left, reading his business card, she was happy to see he became a successful Architect. Looking back, she remembered the twelve-year-old boy who resisted and fought the system.

The authors have shared a comparable story where the mother called the teacher to invite her to her son's graduation. This is a former student who had difficult times in the classroom. The student had written a report that the teacher was the one who made a difference in his life and he never forgot her. The takeaway lesson is: "Our successes may not show up in the classroom. Sometimes they show up when you expect them the least and need them the most."

Reading the chapter on dreams reminded me of my story about dreams where dreams shouldn't just remain dreams; they should become reality whenever possible. Sometimes dreams may seem far-fetched and unreachable but they are attainable. It just means work and time. The authors have also mentioned "through envisioning and expressing, a dream can be manifested into reality by acting upon the intention to bring it forth through faith of believing to receive." This intentionality by envisioning and expressing fulfills the dream that is instilled in our hearts. As a result, it drives our passion to trust, work hard, and achieve our goals. "So, dream big and never give up!"

Those of us who become teachers are answering a call. Teaching is a vocation and not an occupation. I knew I wanted to be a teacher from age seven, but others come to the profession later or even as a second career. What we all have in common is the desire to make a positive impact on the world through the education of our children. When answering a call from God on your life, there will be times when you are weary and discouraged, broken-hearted and beaten down. These moments threaten to turn you away from this call and walk in another direction. The inspiration and encouragement in *TEACHER You are Enough and More* walks alongside teachers as they answer the call to teach and keeps them focused on what is most important.

Hearing from other teachers who know what your life is like makes all the difference. Claire and Karen both have and continue to walk in the path set before them as educators. They know the joys and frustrations that go along with this place we call school. They have been uniquely equipped to help you in your own quest to make a difference in the lives of children. We are called to encourage one another and build up one another. *TEACHER You are Enough and More* does just that for teachers everywhere.

Teachers don't always know where their influence ends. Years later you may be blessed to hear about how you made a difference in the lives of your students. In the meantime, as you fervently put your nose to the grindstone in your work, God has already gone before you to prepare the hearts and minds of the children for whom you have been appointed to serve. As you work, you can be fed by the wisdom in this book.

I highly recommend *TEACHER You Are Enough and More*. Every Christian teacher will find practical and encouraging tips for their teaching lives. When experiencing stress on a rough path, this is a helpful guide to arouse the Spirit, in teachers who make a difference in people's lives. The authors have done a good job writing this book to inspire educators with confirmations, gratitude statements, coping strategies, tools and personal journal writing in completion of the desires and dreams. They have included steps to fulfill your desires and keys to a teacher's success which are essential. Dream big and be persistent. When one dream dies, dream another! Do not give up on your dreams!

I join with Claire and Karen in commending and honoring all the hard-working teachers in service educating our students to benefit our society and our country. Your dedication and hard work does not go unnoticed.

Not many of you should become teachers, my fellow believers, because you know that we who teach will be judged more strictly. We all stumble in many ways. Anyone who is never at fault in what they say is perfect, able to keep their whole body in check.

James 3:1-2 (NIV)

Acknowledgements

We would like to express our gratitude to David Hancock, founder of Morgan James Publishing, and Jim Howard and the design team for their incredible support of our vision for this book.

We are ever so grateful to Terry Whalin, our acquisitions editor, for God putting him in our path to make this book possible. His support and unwavering belief in us made a huge difference in the success of this book.

We are indebted to Anna Floit, our editor, for coming up with wonderful ways of using creative language that is easy to read for you, the reader.

We are proud to present this uplifting book to educators throughout the world.

Introduction

D id you know 40 to 50 percent of teachers leave their profession within five years? What causes teachers to become disheartened in such a short time? Several factors lead to high teacher turnover. In our experience, we have found teacher dissatisfaction stems from having little to no input in the decision-making process. Along with school conditions, student behaviors, discipline policies, and low pay drive teachers to leave the field.

Who spends the most time with children aside from the family? Teachers, of course! We build, educate, enhance, and influence their futures. We know we cannot mend all their hurts, but we can comfort and soothe their emotional needs.

As we teach, words of praise flow from our thoughts through our lips. However, we often forget the Lord's grace and blessings and become carnal-minded, not tapping into the gifts He's given us. Negative thoughts build on each other and manifest darkness. But we get what we think! In the same way, encouraging thoughts build upon each other and manifest positivity. To remain in the light, choose anchor words from Scripture that interrupt negative thinking and align ourselves with our Heavenly Father.

We wrote this book to inspire educators during challenging times. Often in our own careers we longed for a book to support our endeavors and at the same time align our spirits with God. Our aim as authors is to uplift teachers through the teaching profession.

Beginning our day immersed in the Word keeps our minds in the light, remaining positive, and able to handle whatever occurs throughout the day. We understand the demands, stresses, and joys of our profession, having lived it collectively for over fifty years. We hope you enjoy the journey; this book is for you.

Teacher's Prayer

My Heavenly Father,

- Thank you as I start my day with children that I see each child as unique with special talents and great potential.
- Thank you for enlightening me to discipline lovingly and respectfully.
- Thank you that the doors of wisdom are always open to me, for knowledge is silver and wisdom is gold.
- Thank you for giving me patience and understanding to impart critical knowledge onto my students to help them be responsible citizens and achieve their utmost success.
- Thank you for encouraging me to be a good role model who is caring, kind, and respectful to others.
- Thank you for using me as your instrument to make a difference in children's lives.
- (Add your own)

In Jesus' name,
Amen

The Process of Manifesting Your Desires

Our intent is to provide tools for handling stress and persevere through difficult times by staying with our Lord. It's easy to stray from our Heavenly Father when we stay busy trying to make it through the school day. Below are steps to creating and bringing forth your desires and dreams. Be firm and persistent with your intentions.

1. Visualize your desires.

2. Close your eyes and envision in your mind a clear picture of what you want.

3. Express your desire out loud so it will pass through your mouth and heart.

4. See your desire as you express it.

5. Choose one or two statements from the confirmation section of this book to meditate on in the area where you struggle, and focus on these throughout the day.

6. Confirm your desire by writing it down. You can also write your statements on an index card and place it where you see it every day. Repeat these statements several times a day under your breath.

7. Last, believe and receive it. Amen.

Every time you perform these steps you become closer to manifesting your desires. As you anticipate believing and receiving, the key is through faith, believing God has already delivered your desires. Continue to practice these steps, with conviction, until your desire becomes a reality in your life.

Keys To Teacher's Success

- Remain in God's Word.
- Express gratitude.
- Envision and express your desires.
- By faith believe to receive.
- Confirm.
- Write down your desires.

Use these keys to elevate your soul to a positive mindset in achieving your dreams and desires. These will also keep your mind and body balanced and better able to cope with stress.

Teacher

As a teacher, you know your job is not easy, but you've been called and given the gift of teaching.

> *Not many of you should become teachers, my fellow believers, because you know that we who teach will be judged more strictly. We all stumble in many ways. Anyone who is never at fault in what they say is perfect, able to keep their whole body in check.*
>
> James 3:1-2 (NIV)

How does one ignite the love of learning in a child? God has given you the wisdom, responsibility, and knowledge to train students in the love of learning, which you in turn model for your students every day.

> *To know wisdom and instruction; to discern the words of understanding; to receive the instruction of wise dealing, in righteousness, justice, and equity; to give prudence to the simple, knowledge and discretion to the young man.*
>
> Proverbs 1:2-4 (WEB)

Your dedication and hard work do not go unnoticed! Although not all of us can teach Bible principles directly, we can all model and teach them indirectly.

Reading and reflecting on these scriptures leads to stronger faith and love that comes through in your teaching. Therefore, it effortlessly becomes the fruit of your spirit. Our work is taken seriously, for we work directly for God.

Train up a child in the way he should go; even when he is old, he will not depart from it.

Proverbs 22:6 (ESV)

Therefore, my beloved brothers, be steadfast, immovable, always abounding in the Lord's work, because you know that your labor is not in vain in the Lord.

1 Corinthians 15:58 (WEB)

Finally, our focus is on our students' achievement and well-being. We commend all teachers for their tireless efforts in these areas. We want you to be encouraged and inspired daily through the scriptures we provided to do your best and maintain harmony, peace, and balance in your life.

1
Become Your Dream

Teacher, what dream and desire is in your heart? Do you have a dream to fulfill? It is time to set your mind with the intention. How do you make your dream come true? To manifest a desire, you need to have a sense of purpose. In doing so, you attract your wants unto yourself with your thinking, using carefully chosen words and taking the initiative in envisioning, expressing, and writing down your specific desire.

Do you dream of a good school year? What is your plan? By focusing on that plan and creating your path with determination and without deviation or wavering, you turn your wishes into reality. Remain steadfast through the times you feel your desires will never come to pass. As you wait, you might think your wishes could die completely. Be persistent, though. When one dream dies, dream another! Do not give up on your dreams!

How deep is your relationship with God? Keep in mind, we are God's dream and He created us for His purpose to have a relationship with Him through prayer. The intention of prayer drives our purpose. This purpose takes on a deeper meaning when we know we belong to the Holy Father with the intentionality to fulfill the dream He instilled in our hearts. As a result, it drives our passion to work hard to achieve our goals.

Scripture:

> *And the Lord answered me: Write the vision; make it plain on tablets, so he may run who reads it. For still the vision awaits its*

appointed time; it hastens to the end—it will not lie. If it seems
slow, wait for it; it will surely come; it will not delay.

Habakkuk 2:2-3 (ESV)

He said, "Hear now My words: If there is a prophet among you, I,
the Lord shall make Myself known to him in a vision. I shall speak
with him in a dream.

Numbers 12:6 (NASB)

The Lord will fulfill his purpose for me; your steadfast love, O
Lord, endures forever. Do not forsake the work of your hands.

Psalm 138:8 (ESV)

Then he dreamed another dream and told it to his brothers and
said, "Behold, I have dreamed another dream. Behold, the sun, the
moon, and eleven stars were bowing down to me.

Genesis 37:9 (ESV)

Experiences:

How did we fulfill our dreams? We both knew from a young age we wanted to be teachers. When college approached, a friend's mother who was a nurse encouraged Claire to go into nursing. Claire started college thinking she would be a nurse, but the passion was not there. Since kindergarten, her dream was to become a teacher; therefore, she switched her major to Elementary Education. This is when she flourished and enjoyed the course work. Claire is happy in a productive career without regret.

Karen dreamed of being a teacher since second grade as she played school with her brother growing up. Of course, she was always the teacher. Every class she took was for this career, and went on to become not only an elementary teacher but a teacher librarian as well. Karen experiences much success and enjoyment in this profession.

Dreaming and desires are biblical concepts. These come from the Lord. There is nothing wrong with having big goals and asking the Lord to create these desires collectively with Him.

Do you have an assignment? Are you prepared to fulfill it? We believe He has given us a specific assignment to fulfill, and He also has given us the ability to accomplish that assignment using our talents and our determination to complete it. Sometimes we can lose sight of how to achieve our dreams and we must ask God for direction.

Along the way, the Lord moves the right people into our paths to mentor us. We are thankful we are placed on the right road to complete our destiny and are created to help each other to further His kingdom. We live with abundance and prosperity, along with joy, happiness, and good health. We are God's children and every parent wants to see their children succeed.

Confirmations:

- I am fulfilling my dreams.
- I am steadfast with my dream (state your dream).
- I am determined without wavering.
- I am decisive with my intentions in pursuing my goal.
- I am manifesting my dream.

Envision and Express the Following:

- I envision myself living my dream with no doubt.
- I view myself successful in whatever I do.
- I see myself taking steps closer to my dream.
- I perceive myself on the righteous path without fear.
- I see myself planning and staying focused on my desire.
- The enemy will not deceive me.
- My shepherd is leading me to the right path.
- I declare my dreams are coming to pass.
- What is in heaven will manifest itself on earth.
- My shield of faith and the sword, the Word of God, protects me from the enemy.
- I believe and I receive. Amen.

My desires are...

_____

_____

_____

_____

_____

_____

2
Stewardship

We are God's stewards and are responsible for managing what He has given to us, as everything belongs to Him. Our Creator entrusts these things to us and we are accountable for how well we manage them. What are some things God is entrusting to you? For us, this includes our wisdom, relationships, knowledge, time, and our finances. As we oversee a few things with good intention, many things will come our way to bless and enrich our lives.

Teachers are entrusted with the gift of teaching from above. Not everyone is capable of teaching and fulfilling the tasks to meet the needs of the pupils. We are mindful not to abuse the authority and power given to us or cross the line of treating people badly. Through the Holy Spirit, we have the strength and the inspiration to manage our lives obediently for His glory.

Scripture:

His master replied, "Well done, good and faithful servant! You have been faithful with a few things; I will put you in charge of many things. Come and share your master's happiness!"
Matthew 25:21(NIV)

So then each one of us will give an account of himself to God.
Romans 14:12 (ESV)

Commit your work to the Lord, and your plans will be established.
Proverbs 16:3 (ESV)

Let a man regard us in this manner, as servants of Christ and stewards of the mysteries of God. In this case, moreover, it is required of stewards that one be found trustworthy.
1 Corinthians 4:1-2 (NASB)

As each has received a gift, use it to serve one another, as good stewards of God's varied grace.
1 Peter 4:10 (ESV)

Experiences:

Are you a steward of God? Teachers prepare students for the future and the good of the kingdom. We comply and carry on the work without rocking the boat and bringing attention to ourselves; yet we agree there are times speaking out is necessary. We make it work by meeting deadlines and elevating students to work at their greatest potential. It is also about growing as spiritual individuals and refining our character traits through our daily experiences.

We knew teachers who left the building to seek another position or left the system with anger. They would delete or throw out important documentations that made it difficult on other teachers to recreate the plans set for the students. The unaccountable behavior and mismanagement of stewardship is unacceptable. Bad attitudes do not accomplish anything and the cycle accompanies the person into their next position. Teachers are professionals and must conduct themselves with high standards of stewardship, attitudes, and upstanding behavior.

Confirmations:

- I am committed to the work of the Lord as His faithful servant.
- I am a steward of God who has given me the ability to impart wisdom, knowledge, and understanding.
- I am responsible for how I treat others and what I do with what God has entrusted in me.

- I am following the principle of our Lord and managing what He has created.
- I am accountable to our Heavenly Father as the rightful owner of all to receive my reward.

Envision and Express the Following:

- I see myself receiving my inheritance as a good steward.
- I view myself upholding all required of me.
- I see myself working and serving my students for the good of the kingdom.
- I perceive myself growing as a spiritual being through all my experiences.
- I see myself filled with happiness as a faithful steward of God.
- I commit my work to the Lord and my plans are established.
- I receive my gift of teaching with thanksgiving.
- I accept the authority and wisdom that is given to me.
- I praise the Lord that I am used as a vessel to enhance His kingdom.
- We are God's hands to bring forth what He has established.

My desires are...

_____

_____

_____

_____

_____

3
Prayer, Faith and Worship

Prayer and meditation is how we communicate with the Holy Spirit. Believing is faith and worship is praise and gratitude for what we have. We have faith, but sometimes it is blocked by anger, fear, non-forgiveness, and hopelessness. Believing and trusting makes it possible for us to partake of the blessings and grace He has bestowed upon us, without limits. We believe with love and receive our requests without wavering. This does not come easy, and it takes practice to manifest the grace. God cannot do it for us, but works through us as it is up to us to think, speak, and acquire the desires of our hearts.

How important is prayer during your school day? Prayer is important but prayer is not begging and repeating our requests to God. When we ask for a specific need, God hears us and goes to work to make our requests come true. In the meantime, we must have faith, stay in peace, and believe and act upon our desires to make them happen. Think and dream big!

Scripture:

Now faith is the assurance of things hoped for, proof of things not seen.
Hebrews 11:1 (WEB)

All things, whatever you ask in prayer, believing, you will receive.
Matthew 21:22 (WEB)

For nothing spoken by God is impossible.
Luke 1:37 (WEB)

That your faith wouldn't stand in the wisdom of men,
but in the power of God.
1 Corinthians 2:5 (WEB)

He said to them, "Why are you fearful, O you of little faith?" Then
he got up, rebuked the wind and the sea, and there was a great calm.
Matthew 8:26 (WEB)

Experiences:

As we look back, we realize how rough the school year can be. The demands of the administrators, parents, and students forced us to rely on our faith to pull us through as we were feeling down, overwhelmed, frustrated, and depleted. Many lunch breaks were spent discussing our day and taking the time to meditate, pray, and write confirmations in our journals. This act helped us to elevate our thoughts into positive energy. This sustained us throughout the day and pulled us out of excessive complaining and venting.

It is difficult to reverse our negative thoughts from the venting mode during the crux of emotional turmoil. Therefore, we made an agreement that whenever one of us started venting, we would remind each other not to dwell in the act of complaining. Instead, we channeled our thoughts into positive conversation, as complaining takes us deeper into darkness.

Usually by the afternoon, we felt revitalized due to our meditation, gratitude and a moment of silence. We started the rest of the day with renewed energy and hope. We were better equipped to make wise choices as unexpected circumstances and emergencies occurred in our classroom. At the end of the day, we took time to reflect on how prayer and fellowship helped us to overcome challenges confirming our success through our faith in Jesus Christ.

Confirmations:

- I am thankful for knowledge, wisdom, and a sound mind.
- I am trusting of the Lord that He is pulling me through.

- I have faith in receiving the desires of my heart.
- I am victorious.
- I am a righteous person living by faith.
- I am renewed with the Holy Spirit.
- I am thankful for friends who lend an understanding ear.

Envision and Express the Following:

- I see myself receiving the desires of my heart.
- I perceive myself staying in peace while the Lord is working on my behalf.
- I see my requests and desires (state your specific desires) manifesting themselves.
- I view good things coming my way.
- I notice I accomplish my vision and goals.
- I believe and I accept the abundance without wavering.
- I have the inheritance of my Lord.
- My angels are guiding me and my Heavenly Father protects me.
- My mouth professes my faith.
- I serve a big God so I think big and dream big!
- All things are possible through the Holy Spirit.

My desires are...

_____

_____

_____

_____

_____

_____

4
Values

From childhood, values are instilled in us and are part of our everyday teaching. What values are important to you? Do you impart these values in your students? We impart these values in our students whether we realize it or not, and it plays a large role in the development of our students' futures.

In our lives, we uphold the values and principles most important to us. These guiding principles set the tone of expected behavior and attitudes in both students and teachers. In the end, values are just as important as curriculum, as values include fairness and generating new ideas to serve the community. The values we implement drive our society and develop good character.

Scripture:

And as you wish that others would do to you, do so to them.
Luke 6:31(ESV)

How much better it is to get wisdom than gold! And to get understanding to be chosen above silver.
Proverbs 16:16 (NASB)

Pray for us, for we are sure that we have a clear conscience, desiring to act honorably in all things.
Hebrews 13:18 (ESV)

Whoever walks in integrity walks securely, but he who makes his
ways crooked will be found out.

Proverbs 10:9 (ESV)

Who among you is wise and understanding? Let him show by his
good behavior his deeds in the gentleness of wisdom. But if you
have bitter jealousy and selfish ambition in your heart, do not be
arrogant and so lie against the truth.

James 3:13-14 (NASB)

Experiences:

Educational standards place many requirements on teachers for their students to succeed academically. However, implementing social values are just as important. In our experiences, district standards drove our meetings, workshops, and professional developments. We infused these values into our daily teaching as well as our own personal values.

Some students come with a different set of values and it becomes difficult when parents have one set of values and the school has another set. For example, once we had a father who told his child if someone hits you, you hit them back. This did not set well with our school policy when the child retaliated physically with another student on the playground.

Thereafter, to clarify our discipline code we had a meeting with the parents. This made the father angry for he did not agree with our policies. However, we thoughtfully brought the father along in understanding the process of our discipline policy explaining what is fair and equitable to all students. We reminded the parent that violence is not a solution. We do not want to establish aggressive behavior as a pattern to solve problems, but through appropriate communication we can avoid conflicts. Coming to an understanding through collaboration, the father finally accepted the discipline plan.

In conclusion, educating parents is just as necessary as educating students to impart values. Values are important to teach and are taught through different venues such as personal, home, school, and district. Such valuable experiences shape our students, community, and ultimately our society.

Confirmations:

- I am steadfast in teaching important values of life.
- I am fair and equitable.
- I am following God's gentleness and wisdom.
- I am open to the truth and not to arrogance.
- I am in my heart, not blinded by bitter jealously or selfish ambitions.
- I am wiser than gold and my understanding is above silver.

Envision and Express the Following:

- I envision my student's happy and following appropriate behavior values.
- I view myself enhancing my own personal values.
- I see myself with a good attitude as an example for my students.
- I see my school following appropriate values.
- My values make a difference in my students' lives.
- My students are internalizing the values taught.
- My success comes from following God's goodness and guidance
- I conduct myself with integrity.
- Parents understand the values of our school.
- I have a clear conscience and act honorably.
- I have wisdom, knowledge and understanding from above.

My desires are...

_____

_____

_____

_____

_____

5
Gratitude

Practicing daily gratitude is one of the keys to manifesting your desires. It is giving thanks for the things we have received and the appreciation of His grace and blessings. Offering thanks in our prayers daily gets God's attention and brings forth our desires much faster. Do you practice gratitude daily? How important is expressing gratitude? Practicing gratitude and praise opens the door of communication with the Holy Spirit. It is helpful to keep a daily journal of gratitude to get into the habit of being grateful. Therefore, gratitude is the groundwork of all things to come.

Cultivating a spirit of gratitude can bring happiness and joy in our lives. It brings about good experiences and strong relationships, improving health and emotional being. We are better able to deal with adversity as gratitude protects us from envy, jealousy, and developing a hardened heart. Our thoughtful disposition develops our spirit; therefore, our thoughts and spoken words matter.

Scripture:

O give thanks to the Lord, for He is good;
for His lovingkindness is everlasting.
1 Chronicles 16:34 (NASB)

I praise you, for I am fearfully and wonderfully made. Wonderful
are your works; my soul knows it very well.
Psalm 139:14 (ESV)

O Lord, you are my God; I will exalt You,
I will give thanks to Your name; For You have worked wonders,
Plans formed long ago, with perfect faithfulness.

Isaiah 25:1 (NASB)

But thanks be to God that though you were slaves of sin, you became obe-
dient from the heart to that form of teaching to which you were committed,
and having been freed from sin, you became slaves of righteousness.

Romans 6:17-18 (NASB)

Experiences:

Getting out of bed with the spirit of gratitude and thankfulness on daily basis set our day to a good start; praying for the grace of God and His favor to be upon us. In addition, we practiced gratitude driving in our cars on our way to and from school. We prayed before special meetings and teacher-parent conferences that all would go well. For the most part, all did go well with the parents and teachers.

Gratitude is practiced in school. We encourage our students to keep a daily journal of what they are grateful for, in their lives. This is used as a subject for a writing prompt culminating with the students sharing their experiences in class. We found this to be powerful for developing the skills needed to envision and express gratitude bringing the students closer together promoting unity in the classroom.

Some parents come to us with heavy hearts for their kids. Our job required us to put these parents at ease and let them know we understand their children.

Have you ever experienced parents with so much control over their children, afraid to allow their children to be independent? Well, we had several moms and dads who were "Helicopter Parents" and practically lived at our school, following their children everywhere they went. And this continued for many years.

Through working closely with the parents, they gradually released control and became more trusting of the teachers. We encouraged them to keep a daily journal for their kids with gratitude statements. In turn, this practice motivated them to provide many good ideas to benefit all children. Some of these parents now volunteer with activities to help the school, and their commitment is greatly appreciated by the school community. Upon leaving our school, their children had increased confidence and developed a positive self-esteem. These parents expressed gratitude to the teachers for making such a difference in all children's lives.

Confirmations:

- I am grateful for the wisdom to communicate with the parents.
- I have patience and understanding.
- I am grateful for my job, my students, and my school.
- I am grateful for all God has given me.
- I am grateful for energy and vitality.

Envision and Express the Following:

- I visualize myself comforted and uplifted today.
- I see myself taking my time to enjoy teaching.
- I perceive myself safe and secure in my environment.
- I see myself being organized and productive.
- I foresee myself in a bright future.
- I give thanks for my present prosperity.
- My yoke is easy and my burdens are light.
- I not only have enough, but I have more than enough to share and give.
- I give thanks for my family and friends.
- Be thankful for knowing my Holy Father.
- I will remind myself to be in the Word during rough patches and good times.

My desires are...

_____

_____

_____

6

Obedience

Although it is difficult to stay on the right path every day, it is important to be obedient and non-resistant. In the workplace, we face many pressing deadlines, but it is essential to be aware and strive to love each other every day. Do we really have a choice in being obedient and conducting ourselves with integrity? One does have a choice, and disobedience causes pain, grief, and brings discord into our lives.

On the other hand, obedience is the true sign of our love for our Divine Father. The only way to obey and know the Holy Spirit is by listening attentively to the Word. We break the pattern of resistance with a forgiving heart and put our troubles in His hands. Obedience brings blessings and is an important part of the Christian belief by yielding our will to God.

Scripture:

For you were called to freedom, brothers. Only do not use your
freedom as an opportunity for the flesh, but through love serve one
another. For the whole law is fulfilled in one word:
"You shall love your neighbor as yourself.
Galatians 5:13-14 (ESV)

Slaves, obey your earthly masters in everything; and do it, not only
when their eye is on you and to curry their favor, but with sincerity
of heart and reverence for the Lord.
Colossians 3:22 (NIV)

And this is love: that we walk in obedience to his commands.
As you have heard from the beginning,
his command is that you walk in love.

2 John 1:6 (NIV)

Now if you obey me fully and keep my covenant, then out of all
nations you will be my treasured possession.
Although the whole earth is mine.

Exodus 19:5 (NIV)

Experiences:

Have you known people who vent and release their frustrations on you? We have! There are times when we want to vent, gossip, and complain about our workload, but excessive complaining works against us as this is not obedience. The mayhem is a hindrance to our success and it leaves the door ajar for the enemy to work against us. It is up to us how to respond and handle the unexpected. To be obedient is to watch what comes out of our mouths and turn to the Word of God to strengthen our faith.

Over the years, we have seen many teachers and principals come and go. Have you been in a situation in which the staff was so unhappy that it led to a crescendo of inappropriate actions? There is nothing worse than when a faculty turns on each other or against a leader. Then the majority jumps on the bandwagon of judgment and disobedience, creating chaos, as we have witnessed in one of our schools. A sense of emptiness follows and the door pops open for destruction. The situation can turn ugly, with no winners. This is not best for the progress of the students or the school community.

In the end at this school, the bad behavior of adults caused the scores and the moral of the school to tank; and it took years for the school community to recover. In our experience, we have decided it is best not to become part of the annihilator group. In our observation, the more the group expands the more powerful they become, which makes it difficult not to be drawn into the turmoil of emotional frenzy.

We resisted the strong opinions to join the crowd and attend off campus meetings. It is best in times like this to stay focused on our work without unnecessary distractions that deplete us of our energy and cause stress. During this dark period, letters written to the administration revealed hurtful comments. Some teachers experienced feelings of despair, knowing the morale of the school was failing. Through obedience, we endured in keeping our jobs and maintaining stability in the school, and eventually the troublemakers left.

Confirmations:

- I am well able to forgive and overlook other people's weaknesses.
- I am a champion and I let go of anger.
- I am committed to prevailing through love and keeping the Lord's requirements always.
- I am listening to the Word and obeying; therefore, I am blessed.
- I am loved and remain in God's love.
- I am confident our school is turning around.

Envision and Express the Following:

- I visualize myself teaching in front of my class, being obedient.
- I see myself working with my students or children with love.
- I view myself with patience and endurance.
- I see a glimpse of myself living a long, happy life of obeying fully.
- I see myself recognizing and resisting the calamity around me.
- I live life with joy.
- I give and receive love.
- I count my blessings.
- My workload is light and effortless.
- I rebuke the enemy's stronghold.
- I listen and receive the word of God.

My desires are...

_____

_____

_____

7

Receiving

As teachers, we are so busy giving unconditionally it becomes difficult to ask and to receive. We need to calm our minds so we can receive; otherwise, we will miss it. We do not get if we do not ask, but God loves giving to us. Is it possible to receive everything we need? Yes, everything we need is possible from our Heavenly Father. "Therefore, I tell you, whatever you ask for in prayer, believe that you have received it, and it will be yours." Mark 11:24 (NIV).

We ask by faith, we believe, and then we receive! When we stay in faith, God helps us along the way, but our thoughts are important. We need to be still and listen to what He is saying and wants us to do. We are to be thankful and humble to receive the many blessings that are in store for us.

Scripture:

Every good gift and every perfect gift is from above,
and coming down from the Father of lights,
with whom there is no variation or shadow due to change.

James 1:17 (ESV)

This is the boldness which we have toward him,
that if we ask anything according to his will, he listens to us.
And if we know that he listens to us, whatever we ask,
we know that we have the petitions which we have asked of him.

1 John 5:14-15 (WEB)

If you then, being evil, know how to give good gifts to your children, how much more will your Father who is in heaven give good things to those who ask Him!

Matthew 7:11 (WEB)

Praise the Lord! Blessed is the man who fears the Lord, who greatly delights in his commandments! His offspring will be mighty in the land; the generation of the upright will be blessed. Wealth and riches are in his house, and his righteousness endures forever.

Psalm 112:1-3 (ESV)

Experiences:

When you see growth in your students; be thankful and receive the rewards of your labor. Your righteousness is blessed with wealth and riches coming to you and your good intentions are recognized. For example, by the end of the school year, a parent wrote a letter to the principal stating appreciation for the teacher who taught one of her kids how to read. The parent thought at that time, because of the student's slow progress, being able to read was not a possibility. However, the teacher saw the potential and desire in the child to succeed in reading. The teacher felt grateful for receiving such a compliment.

We receive compliments and blessings with grace! We have an overflow of abundance from our Heavenly Father, and we receive it without feeling sheepish. We, as teachers, do not realize the influence we have on our students and parents. Do not take this for granted! When we receive, and accept, more comes our way!

On the other hand, we had leaders and parents who rarely praised the teachers for excellent work and this set the tone for the climate of our school. They maintained a negative attitude that we were not enough and more was required. The work completed is treated as just part of our job so no compliments were necessary.

Yes, these tasks are a part of our job, yet a simple thank you means so much. It increases enthusiasm and the willingness to do more than what is expected. Educators are the same as students needing praise for work well done; hence, the overall school morale is elevated. Ultimately everyone benefits!

Confirmations:

- I am grateful for the success of my students.
- I am grateful my hard work is appreciated.
- I accept compliments, gifts, and blessings coming my way.
- I receive the rewards of my labor.
- I draw love to me.

Envision and Express the Following:

- I see myself living in abundance.
- I view myself relaxed and at peace.
- I recognize myself without lack.
- I notice myself present in the love that surrounds me.
- I see myself meditating and delighted in His Word.
- I accept what the Lord gives me with thanksgiving.
- I receive my requests with gratefulness.
- I receive knowledge and creativity.
- Wealth and riches are in my house with overflowing abundance.

My desires are...

_____

_____

_____

_____

_____

_____

8
Communication

Great things are accomplished through good communication without sarcasm. We converse with people and with God. When we communicate, we not only talk but we also listen to hear other perspectives and not offend other people. How attentively do you listen to others speaking to you? When someone is talking to us and we are thinking about how we are going to respond, we are not listening. Words can hurt or they can encourage. Words are powerful and reflect what is in our minds and hearts. When we speak, we must be aware of our body language and facial expressions, watch the tone of our voices and maintain eye contact when speaking and listening to assure the other person has our full attention. We ought to always have good intentions without judgment or faultfinding.

On the other hand, sometimes people think they are funny when using a sarcastic tone toward others. But often the reverse happens. The receiving person might take this type of talk as an insult or a putdown. Instead, make all conversations straightforward and to the point, but filter bluntness with a polite demeanor. We communicate daily, but using foolish words hinders our success. Ultimately, it is a choice to be mindful and insightful of the feelings of other people with whom we communicate.

Scripture:

Set a guard over my mouth, Lord;
keep watch over the door of my lips.

Psalm 141:3 (NIV)

He who gives an answer before he hears,
it is folly and shame to him.
Proverbs 18:13 (NASB)

My dear brothers and sisters, take note of this: Everyone should be
quick to listen, slow to speak and slow to become angry, because
human anger does not produce the righteousness that God desires.
James 1:19-20 (NIV)

For by your words you will be justified,
and by your words you will be condemned.
Matthew 12:37 (ESV)

A soft answer turns away wrath, but a harsh word stirs up anger.
The tongue of the wise commends knowledge,
but the mouths of fools pour out folly.
Proverbs 15:1-2 (ESV)

Experiences:

Sometimes our communication with students is misunderstood. Once in a small group setting a discussion took place with a student about inappropriate behavior. The student next to him took it personally and thought the communication was directed at him. He asked the teacher for permission to go to the bathroom, pulled out his cell phone and called his mother. He told his mother the teacher was reprimanding him for no reason. Naturally, the parent believed her son.

The mother called the teacher immediately, which took the teacher by surprise and made her defensive, but catching it early prevented the situation from getting out of hand. A discussion with the parent clarified the conversation between the teacher and the other student. It had nothing to do with her child. Because the reprimand was directed to his friend, he decided that it was directed toward both. The incident resolved itself through proper communication with a carefully detailed explanation to the parent. The parent appreciated and understood that her child takes things personally, even at home when conversation is not directed toward him.

Confirmations:
- I am calm and flexible.
- I am a good listener.
- I am balanced and in control.
- I am understanding and patient.
- I am slow to anger and quick to listen.

Envision and Express the Following:
- I view myself as respectful.
- I see myself apologizing when needed.
- I catch myself non-resistant and conforming.
- I see myself protected by my heavenly angels.
- I spot myself guided by my loving Creator.
- I speak clearly and fairly.
- My voice is soft and I speak with a good attitude.
- I communicate clearly and accurately.
- I stop and listen to what is communicated.
- I make wise word choices in dealing with students and parents.

My desires are...

_____

_____

_____

_____

_____

9
Critical Spirit

To pass judgment and find fault is the action of a critical spirit. Finding faults in others is a subconscious means to elevate one's own self-confidence and self-importance. People with critical spirits dwell on the negative, usually unaware of their poor behavior. Teachers are open to criticism from all directions. Criticism can become a bad habit of faultfinding and this pattern needs to be broken and set aside, especially when we are unaware of the other person's condition and intent.

Is constructive criticism beneficial? Yes, sometimes-constructive criticism or feedback is needed and works best when it is about something specific. However, it should be expressed in love to build up a person instead of tearing them down. This is done in the presence of the person and not behind their back. A critical spirit prevents us from following God's plan for our lives and for that reason we keep our heart pure.

Scripture:

Don't judge, so that you won't be judged. For with whatever judgement you judge, you will be judged; and with whatever measure you measure, it will be measured to you.
Matthew 7:1-2 (WEB)

Therefore encourage one another and build each other up, just as in fact you are doing.
1 Thessalonians 5:11 (NIV)

Love never gives up, never loses faith, is always hopeful,
and endures through every circumstance.

1 Corinthians 13:7 (NLT)

Above all, keep loving one another earnestly,
since love covers a multitude of sins.

1 Peter 4:8 (ESV)

Experiences:

There are many causes for a critical spirit. Aside from negativity, it stems from unforgiving or bitterness toward another person. It often comes from immaturity, insecurity, and past hurt. The answer is to renew your mind by showing love, compassion, and encouragement. This is not easy but through practice, it can be achieved. God has given us grace, mercy, and forgiveness, and we thank Him in our journey to overcoming a critical spirit.

People can be very critical of each other. For instance, a teacher was made of fun for the way she dressed and carried herself. This unacceptable, exaggerated rumor inflamed throughout the staff. The critical gossip became pertinacious and amplified unnecessarily. The intolerant attitude got out of hand, and the person involved became offended. The teacher heard about the tittle-tattle through the grapevine and found out who spread the gossip. A conversation followed to clarify the whispers and made it known this type of behavior is unacceptable in the workplace. Be aware of such harsh judgment and how words and actions hurt others.

Confirmations:

- I am courageous and endure through every circumstance.
- I am confident and encouraging.
- I am patient and think positively.
- I am seeing the best in every person.
- I am compassionate and complete through God's grace.
- I am free of all past hurts.
- I am a giver and a helper.

Envision and Express the Following:

- I see people through loving eyes.
- I visualize myself helping other people.
- I notice myself accepting people as they are.
- I see myself forgiving people.
- I find myself with a renewed mind.
- I give and receive the love of God.
- My words are sincere and without sarcasm.
- I remind myself not to judge people.
- I build people up instead of tearing them down.
- I remind myself under all circumstances to stand on the Word of God.

My desires are...

_____

_____

_____

_____

_____

_____

10
Patience

Sometimes we want things immediately. Psalm 75:2 (WEB) says, "I choose the appointed time, I will judge blamelessly." Do you make hasty decisions you later regret? We become impatient and make quick decisions that put us in hot water. But understand, our requests do not necessarily occur in our time, but through trust it will happen in God's time. His timing is perfect and not one minute late. In the meantime, it is important we keep believing, praying, and staying in faith while we align ourselves with our being. Eliminating the barriers and the clutter in our minds hastens our desires to manifestation.

When you think nothing is happening, stay in the Word because this is a test to see if we give up or remain in faith. Lack of patience causes us to miss blessings, but we remind ourselves that patience is love. We trust and believe for God is working in heavenly places on our behalf.

Scripture:

> *But if we hope for what we do not yet have, we wait for it*
> *patiently. In the same way, the Spirit helps us in our weakness.*
> *We do not know what we ought to pray for,*
> *but the Spirit himself intercedes for us through wordless groans.*
> Romans 8:25-26 (NIV)

> *But as for me, I will watch expectantly for the Lord; I will wait for*
> *the God of my salvation. My God will hear me.*
> Micah 7:7 (NASB)

Therefore the Lord waits to be gracious to you, and therefore he exalts himself to show mercy to you. For the Lord is a God of justice; blessed are all those who wait for him.

Isaiah 30:18 (ESV)

Experiences:

Have you had times when you were waiting for your class to calm down so you could start your lesson? How did you feel at that moment? We have all experienced these feelings of anxiety and had to wait patiently for change to occur. Another example is waiting for students to listen to our expectations so optimal learning can take place. Another is to be patient with a student disrupting the class with high demands and to realize we help them choose appropriate behavior. Often our students have issues at home, putting us on high alert to the additional help they might need. Also, it makes us aware to take the time to service their needs and to refer them to the appropriate services available.

A couple of students with discipline issues decided to start a "meow club." This started between two students with cats. When not able to handle a situation from the teacher or other students they would meow to each other and stop listening in class. This attention-seeking behavior went on in the cafeteria, on the playground, in the library, and in the classroom. It gave them an excuse not to complete their work, for both had short attention spans. Eventually the two students took control and the rest of the classroom joined the chorus, meowing to each other. The meowing was loud and contagious. It left the teacher feeling frustrated, defeated, and with a lack of classroom control.

After a while, the rest of the students in the classroom became tired of the running amuck. Support services were set in place to gain control of the classroom. One-on-one and group therapy sessions helped break the reoccurring pattern. Finally, the two students were separated with parental cooperation and consultations. Slowly, by the end of the year, the problem resolved by running its course. This incident took much patience on behalf of the teachers and administration to tone down the chaos brought to our school.

Confirmations:

- I am patient and persevere to handle situations.
- I am protected by my heavenly angels, and my students are on the right path.
- I am confident that help and resources are coming my way.
- I am full of faith that this situation will turn around and is resolved soon.
- I eagerly wait for God to hear my voice.

Envision and Express the Following:

- I see my students focused on their classroom work.
- I view myself moving above and beyond the problem.
- I see my Heavenly Father supernaturally turning the situation around.
- I visualize my students coming to the realization of the unhealthy behavior.
- Kindness and caring are increased toward my students.
- My Heavenly Father is increasing my wisdom and creativity through this calamity.
- I see the big picture of obedience and appropriate behavior of my students.
- My Holy Father assists me always.
- "The Lord is good to those who wait for him, to the soul who seeks him." Lamentations 3:25 (ESV).

My desires are...

_____

_____

_____

_____

11

Respect

What is the culture of your school? Is the persona of your school disciplined and positive for all? Or is it toxic and negative? The culture of the school reflects its student population and its core beliefs. The administration and teachers set the tone for communication with parents and the community, as well as reinforcing values. Everyone who walks through the school doors is worthy of respect and dignity, whether they agree or disagree with the school policies. We regard parents with high esteem and courtesy. We conduct conversations with kindness and grace and without judgment or strong opinions.

In the workplace, we all must be respectful of our colleagues. That means being polite and treating them with dignity, especially when working together to convey ideas and opinions. Good listening skills are necessary to move forward in changing or improving our work as educators. Remember, everyone has good qualities and opinions that deserve to be heard. Be aware of your demeanor in speaking to people and let the person finish speaking without interrupting before we start speaking. Everyone deserves this respect, and you will remain in a positive light as well.

For the most part, our society exhibits a narcissistic behavior and is sensitive to constructive criticism with a self-inflated sense of importance and selfishness. When self-esteem is on the line, parents become intimidated, aggressive, and expect special treatment. As a result, this filters down to the children as they also expect special privileges, making classroom management more difficult.

Have we strayed from our biblical principles of treating other people with respect? How can we change this? We can instill biblical principles in our children through our example and modeling these in our own lives through showing love and respect for everyone. Thus, it brings out the good behavior in our students to improve their life skills.

Scripture:

Let everyone be subject to the governing authorities, for there is no authority except that which God has established. The authorities that exist have been established by God. Consequently, whoever rebels against the authority is rebelling against what God has instituted, and those who do so will bring judgment on themselves.

Romans 13:1-2 (NIV)

Obey your spiritual leaders, and do what they say. Their work is to watch over your souls, and they are accountable to God. Give them reason to do this with joy and not with sorrow. That would certainly not be for your benefit.

Hebrews 13:17 (NLT)

Do not sharply rebuke an older man, but rather appeal to him as a father, to the younger men as brothers, the older women as mothers, and the younger women as sisters, in all purity.

1 Timothy 5:1-2 (NASB)

Show yourself in all respects to be a model of good works, and in your teaching show integrity, dignity, and sound speech that cannot be condemned, so that an opponent may be put to shame, having nothing evil to say about us.

Titus 2:7-8 (ESV)

Experiences:

According to a Harris Poll in USA Today, on January 23, 2014, "students respect teachers dropped from 79 percent to 31 percent."[1] We know this is true because we see it in our schools. Some students are dis-

---

1   Toppo, Greg. "Respect at School in Decline, Survey Shows." USA Today, January 23, 2014.

respectful to their peers and authority due to the lack of adult role models in their lives. Teachers train students in what respectful behavior looks like and what is acceptable. The teacher should show respect always.

Over the years, the number of students using profanity and disrespectful behavior has increased, making it critical for the teacher to model self-control. In one case, the teacher dreaded the last class of the day because a particular student would start eating his leftover lunch. He would share with other students who happened to be allergic to his food. After several attempts of asking him to stop, his parents were contacted due to his not listening.

Initially the parent was just as arrogant and uncooperative, and of course, "the apple does not fall far from the tree." Eventually the parent came around to our way of thinking and spoke to her child about his behavior. In the end, he became more cooperative. He gradually saw the error of his ways and his attitude changed to comply with the teacher's instructions and school rules. He realized he could prevent other students from becoming ill. It was a huge step forward for him to see that his actions do make a difference.

Confirmations:

- I am a model of good works.
- I am teaching my students appropriate behavior and dignity.
- I am forbearing, kind, and firm.
- I am accountable to my actions and behavior.
- I am anointed and fulfilling the will of God.

Envision and Express the Following:

- I see my parents being cooperative and open to constructive criticism for the sake of their child.
- I visualize respect increasing for the work I do.
- I recognize words of praise and appreciation coming from my mouth.
- I see my students elevating to respecting everyone in class.
- I view the teachers in my school being respectful of each other.

- My students are exercising respectful behavior in the classroom.
- My ears are open to hear encouraging words and strategies to improve the classroom behavior.
- My classroom is in control and all is well.
- I honor all in my presence with nobility and respect.

My desires are...

_____

_____

_____

_____

_____

_____

12

Love

God is love and the pulse of life. Whatever you do, do it with love and without expectation. Love is everlasting, and the only thing that separates us from love is fear. We begin by loving from a pure heart and forgiving ourselves by extending love and truth to others, for love is the source of our being. Love is a gift from God. We are grateful we have a Creator who loves us, and we are dear to His heart. No matter how we falter, we are loved, and He gets us back on our feet. In turn, we extend the same love and service to other people.

Have you looked at your inner circle of friends whether at school or at home? Are you sure, they are truly your friends? Be constantly aware of the company you keep, as it will reflect on you becoming like them, be it hot-tempered, judgmental, or quick to anger. Seek wise, disciplined people to associate with and you too will receive rewards of good character. As a result, you count among the wise. Always remember love never ends.

Scripture:

Love is patient and kind; love does not envy or boast; it is not arrogant or rude. It does not insist on its own way; it is not irritable or resentful; it does not rejoice at wrongdoing, but rejoices with the truth. Love bears all things, believes all things, hopes all things, endures all things. Love never ends. As for prophecies, they will pass away; as for tongues, they will cease; as for knowledge, it will pass away.

1 Corinthians 13:4-8 (ESV)

A new commandment I give to you, that you love one another: just as I have loved you, you also are to love one another. By this all people will know that you are my disciples, if you have love for one another.

John 13:34-35 (ESV)

Know, in all these things we are more than conquerors through him who loved us. For I am sure that neither death or life, nor angels nor rulers, nor things present nor things to come, nor powers, nor height nor depth, nor anything else in all creation, will be able to separate us from the love of God in Christ Jesus our Lord.

Romans 8:37-39 (ESV)

Owe no one anything, except to love each other, for the one who loves another has fulfilled the law.

Romans 13:8 (ESV)

Experiences:

Are all students easy to love? Not necessarily. Working with students every day helped us increase and develop the gift of unconditional love. The extent of our love is constantly challenged and tested. Sometimes we have students with severe behaviors who are strong-willed, demanding, and demeaning to teachers and other students. As we see this type of behavior increase in our schools, we continue to discipline with love. This type of behavior teaches us how to love and help the tormented soul.

One time a student, raised by his grandparents, had many behavioral demanding issues brought on by abandonment. Soon the grandmother passed away, leaving the student with emptiness and increased behavioral needs. The teacher working with the student listened with compassion to ease the pain and anxiety the student experienced. Even though the teacher felt overwhelmed and frustrated with the slow progress, the student felt supported and cared for. The teacher was an important component in the student's recovery from the loss and grief. Through God's loving kindness, healing slowly took place. During this lengthy process, all teachers showed love and patience to the student.

Confirmations:

- I give and receive love all the time.
- I am not irritable or resentful.
- I am kind and obliging.
- I am the child of the almighty God.
- I am the loved child of my Heavenly Father.
- I am passing the character trait of love with the highest grade.

Envision and Express the Following:

- I see myself surrounded by the love of God.
- I see myself giving, caring, and a patient person.
- I visualize myself safe and protected by my heavenly angels.
- I see my classroom doors guarded by my warrior angels.
- I envision myself wearing the armor of God to increase love.
- I do not let fear overcome me.
- Love is patient and kind.
- I rejoice with the truth.
- My Creator loves me no matter what.
- Love bears all things.
- My vessel is filled with love.
- Help me, Lord, to further develop the gift of love.

My desires are...

_____

_____

_____

_____

_____

_____

13
Change

Does change bring fear? Change is inevitable, and it moves us forward whether we like it or not. At times, voluntary change and attaining a new position can be positive. But other times, when change happens, as it always does in education, we tend to become fearful and anxious because we do not know where it will lead us. It is another new curriculum and another task we must learn. When we become resistant, life becomes more difficult; therefore, we choose non-resistance to make the transition easier.

When multiple changes occur without the teacher's consent, it is difficult to manage and learn them all at once. Even though change is good, we can become overwhelmed and frustrated to make it all happen. Occasionally we need to voice our concerns to slow it down so we can process the change as it becomes too much too fast. Yet, without change we become stagnate. Of course, it is all in the way we act and respond that makes the difference; but we also trust that the change will help us grow.

Scripture:

Have I not commanded you? Be strong and courageous. Do not be afraid; do not be discouraged, for the Lord your God will be with you wherever you go.
Joshua 1:9 (NIV)

And the world is passing away along with its desires, but whoever does the will of God abides forever.
1 John 2:17 (ESV)

14
Planning

♦

It is four o'clock on Friday afternoon and lesson plans are not in place for next week. Sound familiar? Planning is an important skill for every teacher. Robust short and long-range planning and teaching strategies along with high expectations help us to accomplish goals for our students. Teachers' talents and strengths impact students' learning. Careful planning is an important skill with specific objectives meant to increase school and teacher effectiveness. This is followed by meaningful instruction to apply the strategies planned.

Occasionally, our plans do not go the way we intend them to. Fear sets in, expectations are not met, and teacher effectiveness is questioned. We implement the overall goals and the vision for our students as we hold one another accountable for progress. We also self-reflect on our practices and adjust when necessary to fulfill the plan. During this time, we stay flexible and counsel with our Lord to reveal the right path for growth and development.

Scripture:

Commit to the Lord whatever you do,
and he will establish your plans.
Proverbs 16:3 (NIV)

All this also comes from the Lord Almighty,
whose plan is wonderful, whose wisdom is magnificent.
Isaiah 28:29 (NIV)

In their hearts humans plan their course,
but the Lord establishes their steps.

Proverbs 16:9 (NIV)

Peace I leave with you; my peace I give you.
Not as the world gives do I give to you.
Let not your hearts be troubled, neither let them be afraid.

John 14:27 (ESV)

Experiences:

It is November and Billy is struggling in reading. He knows he will not get up to grade level by June without a specific reading plan. How do we help him? Our responsibility is to collaborate with students like Billy to develop a viable working plan to help him achieve his goal.

Planning is the foundation for a roadmap to success. We teach our students how to plan and set goals to achieve their highest potential. Students are ultimately responsible for their own learning with teacher guidance to motivate them to attain the skill of planning that is used in everyday life. This leads us toward our vision and trust relying on Christ, to take us in the direction we need to go.

Another example of planning together is when the teacher and librarian co-plan and collaborate on lessons together. At first, the teachers are not receptive with this model, but in due time, with the principal's support, most teachers eventually agree. Some teachers love it and cooperate, but some are resistant until they see the value in planning together. They realize it makes perfect sense to the link the students' classroom skills to the information skills being taught in the library. This results in greater understanding and contributes to higher achievement scores.

When teacher librarians and classroom teachers work together planning cooperatively and then teaching together alongside each other as partners, overall achievement gets a boost. The classroom teacher teaches content and the librarian teaches information about literacy and digital learning skills to students. When we practiced this at our school, learning became more powerful and our test scores increased. Careful planning is essential to everything we do as teachers, and it leads us toward success.

Confirmations:

- I am clear with my plans and they lead to success.

- I am motivated to plan for the success of my students and myself.

- I am living a life of plan and purpose, for it is God who works in me.

- I am well able to achieve anything I set my mind to with God's plan for me.

- I am fabulous and an effective teacher!

- I am motivated to plan and collaborate with teachers to expand my knowledge for the benefit of my students.

Envision and Express the Following:

- I view myself successful with my students and in my career.

- I see my goals achieved.

- I feel guided through my plans.

- I envision great things coming my way because my intentions are for my students to prosper.

- I see my Lord establishing my steps.

- All these plans come from the Lord Almighty whose plan is wonderful and whose wisdom is magnificent.

- God is blessing my plans as I prepare for the next steps.

- I go to my source for support.

- I use the Holy Spirit to guide me to become a strong leader for my students.

- I meet all objectives, goals, and expectations.

My desires are...

_____

_____

_____

15
Pride

Pride and arrogance in ourselves can hinder our growth, and it can lead to disappointment and destruction. How often do we struggle with pride? Every day we struggle with desires of the flesh, such as control, conceit, evil thoughts, immorality, theft, wickedness, and envy of others. We need to become humble in spirit and give ourselves a chance to learn from others, as pride is a sin and fouls our ability to make good decisions. Consciously, this needs to be taken seriously, as sometimes we do not even realize when we are prideful.

Immersing and opening ourselves to the wisdom of God puts us in the frame of mind of humility. With humility come honor, wisdom, and reason to be proud of our work. To press on, we need to let go of pride and negative thinking, get into the Word, and connect with our inner being.

Scripture:

Do nothing out of selfish ambition or vain conceit.
Rather, in humility value others above yourselves.
Philippians 2:3 (NIV)

Pride goes before destruction, and a haughty spirit before a fall.
Proverbs 16:18 (NIV)

When pride comes, then comes disgrace,
but with the humble is wisdom.
Proverbs 11:2 (ESV)

For by the grace given to me I say to everyone among you not to
think of himself more highly than he ought to think,
but to think with sober judgment, each according to the measure
of faith that God has assigned.
Romans12:3 (ESV)

Experiences:

We all get arrogant at times. We see some teachers try to outshine each other and look down on their colleagues as incompetent compared to themselves. They tend to dominate and compete, join every committee, and volunteer for tasks. Because they process information quickly, at times, they come off as rude and demeaning. That type of person tends to be full of fear, insecure, controlling, and prone to illnesses. At first, we are stunned, wondering why this person can treat us the way they do, and we don't know how to handle it. We do not react immediately but take the time to assess the encounter.

Have you worked with someone with a type A personality? We all know someone like this, as all schools have this type of personality on staff. However, we do not take this personally. We move faster ourselves and are brief with our communications with them. Other ways of dealing with this type of personality are to approach topics directly, respect their time, and be honest in our approach with them. Understand that success and competition motivates them; therefore, remove yourself from that before it becomes hurtful. Keeping this is mind; we look within ourselves and take the time to examine our own behavior. In communicating with others, we are aware of our need for humility and sensitivity, and we align ourselves with the Holy One.

Confirmations:

- I am polite and honest in my intentions.
- I am humble in spirit and proud of my work for God.
- I am full of good intentions for the good of the whole.
- I am not proud, but willing to learn from others.
- I am equal to my colleagues, no more or no less.

Envision and Express the Following:

- I see the hand of God guiding me through tough situations.

- I take a glimpse of myself increasing with humility.

- I view my enemy with honor and grace.

- I see myself respectful of others.

- I envision myself completing my assignment.

- My thoughts are unpretentious.

- My behavior is modest and honest when dealing with my colleagues.

- I work with honesty.

- I acknowledge the wisdom of other people with which I can increase my own knowledge.

- I do nothing out of selfish ambition or vain conceit.

- I think with sober judgment.

My desires are...

_____

_____

_____

_____

_____

_____

16
Self-Control

How does one define self-control? It is the ability to control emotions and feelings and is a trait hard to fully achieve; we are constantly striving to master this in our own body and spirit. Staying on task can be difficult because of everyday happenings coming into our lives. Is self-control mentioned in the scripture? Self-control is one of the fruits of the Spirit that we should live by and practice daily.

One thing we can do to help us gain self-control when teaching is by taking the time to meditate, thereby calming and putting ourselves in control of our being. It is essential to forgive ourselves when we fail to practice self-control so that we can move on and vow to do better with our future endeavors. We keep our goals and values at the forefront to resist the temptations that occur along the way.

God wants us to live an abundant and fulfilled life. Self-discipline is necessary to achieve a healthy, happy life. Keep our hearts pure, have will-power, watch our words, and keep our desires under control to receive His glory and goodness.

Scripture:

For this very reason, make every effort to supplement your faith with your virtue, and virtue with knowledge, and knowledge with self-control, and self-control with steadfastness, and steadfastness with godliness, and godliness with brotherly affection, and brotherly affection with love.

2 Peter 1:5-7 (ESV)

For God gave us a spirit not of fear
but of power and love and self-control.
2 Timothy 1:7 (ESV)

But I discipline my body and keep it under control,
lest after preaching to others I myself should be disqualified.
1 Corinthians 9:27 (ESV)

But the fruit of the Spirit is love, joy, peace, patience,
kindness, goodness, faithfulness, gentleness, self-control;
against such things there is no law.
Galatians 5:22-23 (ESV)

A man without self-control is like a city broken into
and left without walls.
Proverbs 25:28 (ESV)

Experiences:

Students, as well as adults, can stress and exhibit out of control behavior. Some students just do not have self-control and teachers are left to manage their disruptive behavior without much support. What can we do? When we have students, who are out of control, we can take the time to talk about character traits and how to treat each other kindly. We remind ourselves to use the fruits of the spirit indirectly in teaching our students, and get them back on track by using character trait activities and exercises.

We once had a student who would run around the classroom during lesson time in reaction to the stress of the assignment. This left the student in fight-or-flight behavior with no coping skills and no self-control. The student would not listen to any person of authority, and the adults were frustrated by the lack of control. The only thing we could do was remove the student from the group, eliminating the audience. To keep this student engaged, we provided technology programs and forms of physical motor movements. Changing the tasks using short periods of work time helped with the attention span. The behavior was continuous throughout the year and did not improve until the student moved, thus providing what we call a "Geographical Cure."

Confirmations:

- I am in control of my thoughts, emotions, and my actions.
- I am in control of my mouth and what I say.
- I am in control of my behavior.
- I am in control of how I treat others.
- I am fully persuaded.
- I am in agreement with my Lord.

Envision and Express the Following:

- I see myself in control in difficult times.
- I view myself taking deep breaths to balance myself.
- I hear myself counting backward from 10 to 0.
- I envision myself communicating with clear, concise words.
- I see myself being mindful of what I say.
- I visualize myself in the other person's point of view.
- When hard to control a behavior, I will remove myself from the situation and walk away.
- I will let my Father take control and advise me.
- I leave my troubles in God's hands.
- All is well and under control.
- I accept the circumstance and work on rising above it.

My desires are...

_____

_____

_____

_____

17

Stress

While teaching, stress creeps in and can be debilitating, especially if you are a worrier. Stress can be emotional, physical or mental. Our thinking is not clear when we are stressed and everything becomes unraveled. It causes us to do and say things we would not normally do or say. A feeling of unrest and turmoil is experienced. We may even feel tension and become quite ill.

Can we ease the tension? Scripture has a lot to say about the subject of stress giving us coping skills to ease the tension. Tension is replaced with comfort, happiness, and peace through renewal of the mind and practicing gratitude and thanksgiving. Trust that God, through prayer, will supply all our needs. We can also relieve the stress by doing physical activities such as taking a walk, riding our bikes, listening to music, and meditating. Find what works best for you by taking a break and getting your body and soul in balance.

Scripture:

I keep my eyes always on the Lord.
With him at my right hand, I will not be shaken.

Psalm 16:8 (NIV)

Be on your guard; stand firm in the faith;
be courageous; be strong.

1 Corinthians 16:13 (NIV)

But those who hope in the Lord will renew their strength.
They will soar on wings like eagles; they will run
and not grow weary, they will walk and not be faint.

Isaiah 40:31 (NIV)

Stand firm, and you will win life.

Luke 21:19 (NIV)

Blessed is the man who trusts in the Lord, whose trust is the Lord. He
is like a tree planted by water, that sends out its roots by the stream,
and does not fear when heat comes, for its leaves remain green, and is
not anxious in the year of drought, for it does not cease to bear fruit.

Jeremiah 17:7-8 (ESV)

Experiences:

Stress is a result of the fear of not being able to handle the pressure and demands of work, family, and life. We fail to trust God to provide for all our needs. Teachers are constantly bombarded into believing that they are not enough and could do more causing immeasurable stress. To cope, we put it into God's hands to carry us through instead of taking it into our own hands. One of the keys is to identify the stress factor then forgive and let it go. Carrying the stress for too long can lead to serious illness and the imbalance of the mind and spirit.

When not handled well, stress can be so severe that it unleashes itself in our body. One year when daily observations started, many teachers became weary. Coping skills vary from person to person and are critical in handling overwhelming stress. One teacher was diagnosed with the beginning stages of breast cancer and four months later came down with pneumonia that lasted over six months.

This teacher felt stressed and run down going to radiation every day before school, causing her to feel tired and depleted. Nevertheless, she did not miss a day of school. During these two serious illnesses, prayer and believing that God was restoring her health, along with reading healing scriptures, helped the recovery. Also, she listened to soft, calming, uplifting music and watched comedies to renew her spirit. In due time, this teacher fully recovered and her health restored. We saw this type of stress in teachers' year after year. Therefore, it is critical to hold steadfast in the Word and increase our faith to withstand the pressure and demands of life.

Confirmations:
- I am free of all self-limiting beliefs.
- I am fulfilled and living a life of purpose.
- I am managing stress efficiently.
- I am perfectly healthy in mind, body, and spirit.
- I am beautiful and resilient.

Envision and Express the Following:
- I imagine myself trouble free.
- I feel my body relaxing.
- I see myself in my comfortable and happy place.
- I view myself healthy, fit, and strong.
- I see myself taking the time without being rushed.
- I look and feel wonderful.
- I pace and manage my time appropriately.
- I take breaks without guilt.
- I calm myself down by breathing deeply and crossing the mid-line.
- I can work at my own pace peacefully.

My desires are...

_____

_____

_____

_____

18
Integrity

Integrity is a value that is important in our schools. How does integrity play in our lives? Integrity is doing the right thing, being honest with moral uprightness. We strive always to be sincere and truthful as humans in every aspect of our lives. We are role models to our students and they are watching us. Parents, other teachers, and administrators are watching as well.

Integrity develops consistency of what is fair, right, and just. This character trait is important to instill into our students, as they want to know they can trust us to follow through with our promises. Jesus was sent as a role model to show us how to demonstrate all the promises of God. In that event, we are strong role models to our students as we become strong in our own character.

Scripture:

Whoever walks in integrity walks securely,
but he who makes his ways crooked will be found out.
Proverbs 10:9 (ESV)

Finally, brothers, whatever is true, whatever is honorable,
whatever is just, whatever is pure, whatever is lovely,
whatever is commendable, if there is any excellence,
if there is anything worthy of praise, think about these things.
Philippians 4:8 (ESV)

By this I know that you delight in me: my enemy will not shout in triumph over me. But you have upheld me because of my integrity, and set me in your presence forever.

Psalm 41:11-12 (ESV)

The aim of our charge is love that issues from a pure heart and a good conscience and a sincere faith.

1 Timothy 1:5 (ESV)

But hospitable, a lover of good, self-controlled, upright, holy, and disciplined.

Titus 1:8 (ESV)

Experiences:

At our school, integrity is very important in professional developments, trainings, and in-services. It is revisited frequently with teachers and students. When it came to our state testing, we had much training around ethics and keeping the integrity of the assessments. We are requested to sign documents verifying we understand the rules and regulations of administering the tests. We instilled this in our students as well.

To have integrity is important as we aim high to conduct ourselves honorably, justly, and with commendable character. Thereby, we pass it on to our students and people around us. Integrity is one of the most critical qualities a teacher should possess and is developed through promoting fairness and morality. To do just and what is right delights our Lord.

One year during a book fair in the library, a student found a five-dollar bill on the floor. Instead of keeping the money, he gave it to the teacher. Later, the rightful owner returned to claim the money and was very appreciative to get the bill back. This is an ideal teachable moment in which integrity is applied and used in everyday life. The honest student is praised for his integrity and trustworthy character. Because of the noble action, he received a free book. These honorable behaviors are always recognized and used as examples of high integrity. We stop and take the time when opportunity occurs to instill the character traits in our students to develop the fruit of the Spirit.

Confirmations:

- I am honest and trustworthy.
- I work hard and have a good conscience.
- I am humble and I walk justly with God.
- I am consistent.
- I am a good role model to my students.

Envision and Express the Following:

- I see myself operating with integrity.
- I catch myself doing right and speaking truthfully.
- I see myself reviling with good behavior in Christ.
- I visualize myself walking securely.
- I imagine myself acting truthful and commendable.
- I do my job with integrity.
- I do to others as I wish that others would do to me.
- My Holy Father works in me, both to His will and good pleasure.
- I walk with the Lord and keep my path righteous.
- My behavior is pleasing to God and I am upheld in His presence forever.
- I do my work with a clear conscience.

My desires are ...

_____

_____

_____

_____

_____

_____

19
Endurance and Perseverance

Endurance leads to growth in both character and hope. Endurance is needed when we are distressed or going through hardships. Teaching is a test of endurance and of giving unconditional love. How do you handle trial and tribulations? Trial and tribulations are inevitable but we persevere with a determination to stay steady and anchored. We keep our eye on the Lord with hope that He will help us rise despite difficult circumstances.

Without hope we give up. We make the choice to be resilient and have fortitude with the ability to resist, withstand, recover, and to remain active during the course with strong faith. Obstacles spring up in our path but are an antidote to refine our rough edges, sending us on our way to success. We give up the "poor me" attitude and hold onto hope.

Scripture:

But they who wait for the Lord shall renew their strength;
they shall mount up with wings like eagles;
they shall run and not be weary; they shall walk and not faint.
Isaiah 40:31 (ESV)

Do not be conformed to this world, but be transformed by the
renewal of your mind, that by testing you may discern what is the
will of God, what is good and acceptable and perfect.
Romans 12:2 (ESV)

But the one who stands firm to the end will be saved.
Matthew 24:13 (NIV)

20

Discipline

Without classroom discipline, no learning takes place; therefore, it is important to establish routines that all students will understand and can discern from right or wrong. Discipline is a life skill and the training of self-control starts early in life. Self-control starts with self-respect, following principles instead of one's own desires.

Is discipline painful? Yes, it is painful rather than pleasant, but is an expression of love to protect children from getting deeper in trouble and a way to keep them on track. The product of good behavior is the gift of the fruits of the Spirit. Discipline teaches obedience and we are compelled to be consistent with our discipline methods. We press onward with firm discipline, as an undisciplined mind leads to unhappiness and depression.

Scripture:

For the commandment is a lamp and the teaching a light,
and the reproofs of discipline are the way of life.
Proverbs 6:23 (ESV)

Fathers, do not provoke your children by anger by the way you treat
them. Rather, bring them up with the discipline
and instruction that comes from the Lord.
Ephesians 6:4 (NLT)

Discipline your son, and he will give you rest;
he will give delight to your heart.
Proverbs 29:17 (ESV)

For the moment all discipline seems painful rather than pleasant,
but later it yields the peaceful fruit of righteousness
to those who have been trained by it.
Hebrews 12:11 (ESV)

Experiences:

Our heart sank when a student we just reprimanded walked out of our classroom toward the principal's office. Every day we deal with student discipline and drama. Some students are more difficult than others, taking the liberty of accusing the teacher or other students to harm them. It becomes blown out of proportion, leaving the teacher on pins and needles. Many times, the school security and the police are involved to conduct further investigation. The teacher is viewed guilty instead of given the benefit of the doubt.

Furthermore, the aggressive behavior is a way to interrupt teaching and takes time away from other students to learn in the classroom. Often, it is a way of gaining attention. Frequently some students lie; the child comes first and the student is believed instead of the adult. The student takes control and knows they have the upper hand, leaving the teacher feeling powerless and defeated.

What do you do when a student brings a gun to school in his backpack? An incident took place in the cafeteria when a pupil brought a gun to school. He pulled it out during lunchtime to show it to another student and bragged about it. The kids in the cafeteria notified the teacher on duty and the gun was removed after determining it was not loaded. Even though the teacher had prior gun training, this teacher was still under investigation for handling the gun. While under inquiry, the teacher could not see students until the situation cleared. Meanwhile, the student received a serious consequence. This is when our strength, integrity, and faith are challenged. Fear becomes real and overpowers our thinking often, causing us to make poor choices. Then we let go and give it to God to handle and trust that all works out well in the end.

Guns have no place in the school setting, even for teachers to protect themselves. We know some school districts are heading in that direction, but we feel that is not practical or safe with a classroom full of children. Leave the school security in the hands of the trained personnel, who do it best.

Confirmations:

- I am strong and enhancing my values daily.
- I am restored to my integrity in good standing.
- I am a winner.
- I am not ashamed, for I fear not.
- I am disciplined and zealous because of God's love.

Envision and Express the Following:

- I visualize myself surrounded by the love of the Holy Spirit.
- I see myself back in the classroom teaching.
- I perceive myself forgiven and restored.
- I see my spirit uplifted to the joy of teaching again.
- I envision the heavenly light all around me.
- I call upon the angels in heaven to help me.
- God is good, acceptable, perfect, and will see me abound.
- My Lord is my vindicator and upholds me in the palm of His hands.
- My faith is strengthened.
- I have faith that all is well.

My desires are...

_____

_____

_____

_____

_____

21
Setting Goals

Setting goals are important and something all teachers must do as part of the job requirement. There is much pressure and fear placed on teachers to set lofty goals that are not practical for their student's achievement. How crucial is setting goals? Attainable goals are essential for students to make academic progress but there is often a push to write unattainable goals.

At the end of the year when the students haven't attained the set goals, teachers are penalized, which is reflected in their final evaluation. To that end, when setting and implementing goals ask for guidance. Proverbs 16:9 (ESV) says, "The heart of a man plans his way, but the Lord establishes his steps." We remember just because we have done our goal planning does not mean it is aligned with God's desire for us. Prayer is necessary prior and during goal setting.

Scripture:

But as for you, be strong and do not give up,
for your work will be rewarded.
2 Chronicles 15:7 (NIV)

Trust in the Lord with all your heart, and do not lean on your own
understanding. In all your ways acknowledge him,
and he will make straight your paths.
Proverbs 3:5-6 (ESV)

There is no fear in love; but perfect love casts out fear, because fear has punishment. He who fears is not made perfect in love.

1 John 4:18 (WEB)

May he give you the desire of your heart and make all your plans succeed.

Psalm 20:4 (NIV)

Experiences:

There is much demand placed on teachers to bring up test scores. There is also pressure with excessive testing of students to get quality data to guide teaching instruction. Teacher performance is based on student data results. We have become a data-driven society to the point at which the social and emotional needs of a child are sometimes set aside. Yes, data is important; but we must consider the emotional needs and the developmental level of a child, thereby affecting achievement performance.

The trend is to have kindergarteners reading at a higher level as they enter first grade. The question is, how hard and how far do we push these kids? Is this necessary? What are the parents' responsibilities? A partnership between the parents and the teacher is essential at this age level. Parents must read to their children to reinforce reading skills. These high expectations are not achieved by every child by the end of kindergarten. Physical, emotional, and maturational levels prevent some students from meeting the goal. We must allow kids to grow at their level of maturation instead of placing constant pressure on the teacher to bring up the reading level.

The teacher's evaluation scores reflect the student's performance, and this is difficult when the teacher is working in a low-performing school. This is not going to make the children learn any faster. In the long run, it hurts their self-esteem. In your heart, in spite of all the pressures, choose goals that are practical and guided by the Spirit. At the end, you will shine!

Confirmations:

- I am motivated to align my goals with God's plan.
- I am committed to setting realistic goals for my students.

- I am confident that all things are achieved according to the Lord's plan.
- I am an accomplished teacher.
- I am called to God's love and purpose.

Envision and Express the Following:

- I visualize my goals are accomplished.
- I see myself growing in goal setting skills as I teach my students.
- I perceive my students' emotional needs and academic skills improved.
- I envision love driving all fear away.
- I observe God in all things directing my path, and I am not leaning unto my own understanding.
- My goals are realistic and completed.
- No fear will stand in my way.
- I persevere to see my goals accomplished with humility.
- I have faith that my students will achieve the expected goals.
- My vision is clear and I stay on the path.

My desires are...

_____

_____

_____

_____

_____

_____

22
Observation and Evaluation

Observation and evaluation is measuring teacher effectiveness and performance. It helps to identify strengths, weaknesses, and areas for growth. It is expected to have clear standards of performance to meet the needs of our students. Is it important to review often the students' progress? Review, monitor, and discuss students' growth is important to make sure they are on target to achieve their learning goals.

Students use strategies to accomplish their individual learning objectives and show their learning of content through speaking and writing. Teachers gather evidence based on data tracking using meaningful feedback to enhance learning. This is a time to stay close to God's strength and guidance to meet the standards. Finally, specific teaching content is measured and assessed through observation and evaluation of the teacher's understanding of effective practices set in place by the school and the district.

Scripture:

Give instruction to a wise man, and he will be still wiser;
teach a righteous man, and he will increase in learning.
Proverbs 9:9 (ESV)

That the wise man may hear, and increase in learning;
that the man of understanding may attain to sound counsel.
Proverbs 1:5 (WEB)

The mind of the prudent acquires knowledge,
and the ear of the wise seeks knowledge.
Proverbs 18:15 (NASB)

Our people must also learn to engage in good deeds to meet pressing
needs, so that they will not be unfruitful.
Titus 3:14 (NASB)

Experiences:

In our experience, observations become more difficult and challenging almost daily. The stakes have never been higher. Guideline handbooks of best academic practices containing prescribed language and a mandated curriculum has made us more like cookie cutters or robots with little creativity left.

If prescribed language was not used in our lessons, we were rated lower. The students' behavior was also considered and was reflected in the overall evaluation. For example, the student's lack of cooperation lowered the evaluation scores. This resulted in accelerating the feeling of anxiety and stress for the teacher.

Expectations for building lesson plans required the use of strict prescribed standards without deviation, leaving no flexibility. Fear became prevalent among teachers with a sense of competition. We see many teachers walking down hallways with tears in their eyes because they feel inadequate and incompetent. And that is not ok.

Evaluations are important as our salaries are based on student achievement and student evaluations. Coaches are assigned to each teacher to refine the skills needed to attain goals and lesson delivery, with optimal timing to ensure student-to-student collaboration and work time. Every section of the lesson delivery is measured, for example, timing how long the students are sitting on the carpet in front of the whiteboard receiving instructions. At the end of each lesson, the summary is also timed as it has to be quick or the teacher is penalized.

This coaching model is time consuming and specific to a goal, and we felt spoon fed and babysat every step of the way, especially the seasoned teachers. The observation is such an overload and we did not feel we were trusted to do our jobs. We are excessively coached to attain top scores in both our observations and in student achievement. As a result, this is one of the contributing factors causing teacher shortages for many teachers are evaluating each other while some are pulled away from the classroom to perform administrative type duties. As a result, quality time is taken away from educating students causing frustration adding to the number of teachers leaving the profession. The question is, how far should teachers be pushed? Teachers and students should not be pushed to the breaking point for "you can't get blood from a turnip!"

The End of the Year Conversations with the administration discussed the teacher's overall performance level throughout the year. The final report includes a long list of evaluation criteria that is met by the teacher. Points are taken away for not meeting lofty goals, classroom management, learning environment, using technology, collaboration, next steps, and other matters.

Some teachers did not meet the criteria and were placed on a plan of improvement. Overall, for the most part, teachers achieved what was prescribed. By the end of the year most teachers felt depleted and burned out from unnecessary and excessive pressure from the detailed process. Yet others were left with resentment and overwhelming feelings of not being up-to-par.

In your heart at the end, you know you have done your best all year. Creating strong bonds with your students is an act no one can measure or evaluate. You know you are a teacher who makes a difference!

Confirmations:

- I am rising above the given circumstances and let my Holy Father be my guide.
- I am gifted with the blessing of being an empowered teacher through the guidance of the Lord.
- I am working for God to expand His kingdom.
- I am a highly qualified teacher with excellent intentions.
- I am special and unique.

- I am important and accountable in my performance.
- I am the head and not the tail.
- I am highly encouraged and valued.
- I am a child of almighty God who sees me through all things.

Envision and Express the Following:

- I envision myself with high evaluation marks at the end of the year.
- I visualize myself elevated in the teaching profession.
- I know that I am fulfilling God's work.
- I see myself with no fear, worry, or anxiety.
- I have a glimpse of everything working for my good.
- I know that in my heart God is fighting the battles for me.
- I will not give up!
- My students' achievements and my evaluation will not dictate who I am.
- My goals are achieved and I am complete.
- My ratings and evaluations are exceedingly effective.
- Rewards, gifts, and stipends are coming my way!

My desires are...

_____

_____

_____

_____

_____

_____

23
Manipulation

We have all met a manipulative personality in our life. What is a manipulative personality? There are many types; some are aggressive and some are sneaky. Usually, manipulators exhibit arrogant, narcissistic behaviors that lack empathy. They are somewhat self-absorbed, selfish, and consumed with anxiety. They seek control of other people to get their own way, yet their behavior comes off as being completely normal. First, they gain the trust of the person making them feel respected when just the opposite is happening. They also tend to use people so they can get ahead to the point of being dishonest, or at least not telling everything they know.

Are you a trustworthy person who is easily manipulated? Often it takes a while for a trustworthy person to realize they are being manipulated and taken advantage of for the other person's benefit. Occasionally these types of maneuvers happen in our schools. During these trying times, strong emotions surface, resulting in feelings of hurt and anger.

This brings us to the heart and trust of our relationship with God. We surrender the problem and let Him take care of us so we may be safe. Our goal is always to have healthy and honest conversations with people for the benefit of humanity in hope eventually all comes out for the good.

Scripture:

But understand this, that in the last days there will come times of difficulty. For people will be lovers of self, lovers of money, proud, arrogant, abusive, disobedient to their parents, ungrateful, unholy, heartless, unappeasable, slanderous, without self-control, brutal,

not loving good, treacherous, reckless, swollen with conceit, lovers
of pleasure rather than lovers of God, having the appearance of
godliness, but denying its power. Avoid such people.
2 Timothy 3:1-5 (ESV)

Beware of false prophets, who come to you in sheep's clothing
but inwardly are ravenous wolves.
Matthew 7:15 (ESV)

For such persons do not serve our Lord Christ, but their own appetites,
and by smooth talk and flattery they deceive the hearts of the naive.
Romans 16:18 (ESV)

And no wonder, for even Satan disguises himself as an angel of light.
2 Corinthians 11:14 (ESV)

And Jesus answered them, "See that no one leads you astray."
Matthew 24:4 (ESV)

Experiences:

It is Thursday morning and another faculty meeting to attend. A new concept is brought to the attention of the faculty, followed by a discussion and vote whether we adopt this new program in our school. It is necessary for teachers to buy into adopting this concept before implementing it, even though the concept is encouraged from the top down. We are made to believe it is all up to us to make the choice. But, it is all manipulated ahead of time to pass this directive. Most teachers are compelled to vote against it, thinking it is something else on their plates, but voted for it for fear of repercussions suspecting it is directed from the top.

Manipulation is evident throughout many meetings, but knowing this, silence among the faculty prevailed. Occasionally the faculty did put their foot down. They voted against the directive but usually it came back for a vote again where it is tweaked somewhat, but basically the same. Teachers are made to believe they have a voice. Despite the deception, they work hard to implement the concept to make it a success. Overall, we find teachers are resilient, obedient, compliant, and compassionate to their work. Foremost, they always keep in mind the students and community they serve.

Confirmations:

- I am proud to serve students despite deception.
- I am aware of manipulation and I will not be lead astray.
- I am aware of wolves in sheep's clothing.
- I am faithful in Christ Jesus to lead me in the right direction.
- I am honest and respectful in my dealings.

Envision and Express the Following:

- I see myself being compliant and working for the good of all.
- I envision listening and obeying to God's plan.
- I see myself cooperating with my Lord's instruction.
- I visualize understanding the directive from the top.
- I discern comfort is mine when I know I am manipulated.
- I will not be deceived.
- I rejoice with the truth.
- I will make directives work for the benefit of all students.
- My spirit is strengthened by the grace of God.
- I forgive the manipulative behavior.

My desires are...

_____

_____

_____

_____

_____

24

Power of Words

The words we choose to communicate are powerful, positive or negative, so choose your words wisely. Are you aware of the words you speak? Be careful as they can build up or tear down a person.

Do you take part in idle talk? Careless talk can end up in regret. Excessive babbling keeps us from listening and discerning the truth. Let your tongue speak the language of truth to keep yourself out of trouble, avoiding manipulative and belittling inferences.

As educators, we speak words of encouragement to our students, giving them confidence and inspiration, thus motivating them to their highest level of achievement and emotional abilities. Words have strength and power. Words should always be used with kindness and respect, aligned with our inner awareness and sincerity.

Scripture:

Your word is a lamp to guide my feet and a light for my path.
Psalm 119:105 (NLT)

Let no corrupting talk come out of your mouths,
but only such as is good for building up, as fits the occasion,
that it may give grace to those who hear.
Ephesians 4:29 (ESV)

If you want to enjoy life and see many days, keep your tongue from
speaking evil and your lips from telling lies. Turn away from evil
and do good. Search for peace, and work to maintain it.
1 Peter 3:10-11 (NLT)

Too much talk leads to sin. Be sensible and keep your mouth shut.
Proverbs 10:19 (NLT)

In the beginning was the Word, and the Word was with God,
and the Word was God.
John 1:1 (NIV)

Experiences:

Over the course of the years, incidents have occurred when our choice of words was critical. We treaded lightly, carefully, and gently. Once, a meeting was held to share test results with the parents of an adopted child. The scores, along with the teacher's observations, revealed that their child performed in the low-range academic areas. The father had a difficult time accepting the results of the evaluation, so he began shouting, confronting, and questioning the teacher's qualifications. The teacher kept a cool head, sensitive to the father's concern, and gently shared the documentation and test results.

After careful explanation of the test results along with the body of evidence, the teacher then chose her next words with purpose, putting the father at ease. The parent finally admitted he was disappointed to hear of the child's low performance, in spite of all the interventions set in place. The father finally accepted and realized the test score was commensurate with the child's performance.

The power of words can convey different meanings. For example, many students take misunderstood words and conversations home to parents that lead to clarification of what was said and meant. As usual, the teacher is always the one defending and softening the conversation with carefully chosen words. The students have a different view of what is said, and the conversation can become exaggerated and misconstrued causing parents to become angry. Accordingly, "Let your speech always be gracious, seasoned with salt, so that you may know how you ought to answer each person." Colossians 4:6 (ESV).

Confirmations:

- I let my words come from my heart and be mindful of the person.
- I am wise in my speaking and my tongue commands knowledge.

- I am gracious, kind, and caring in my speech.
- I am always building up and not tearing down people.
- I am gentle and soft with my voice.

Envision and Express the Following:

- I catch my tongue guarded against hurtful words.
- I view myself speaking no evil and no lies coming out of my lips.
- I practice saying uplifting words.
- I see and hear a soft tone of voice.
- I see a pleasant expression on my face.
- I catch myself before I speak.
- I speak words of encouragement, wisdom, and knowledge.
- I shield my mind from wandering thoughts.
- I release all negative thoughts and angry words.
- I rejoice for my great reward is in heaven.

My desires are...

_____

_____

_____

_____

_____

_____

25

Blessings and Grace

The blessings and the grace of God is a gift of love for us all, despite our sins. We seek and believe through faith to access His grace. Not believing blocks the blessings and rejects all that is in store for us. We accept the goodness, kindness, and good will through believing and receiving in Jesus Christ.

Do teachers go through hardships? Have you wondered why? There are many reasons. Our Savior's perfect plan includes what we think are hardships, but are blessings in disguise and work for our benefit. They mold us into the teachers He wants us to be.

We exercise faith through daily prayer with humility and gratitude, manifesting our desires and the favor of God. Do you take the time to be thankful daily? Taking the time to be thankful for blessings and the gift of grace that is already there should be second nature. Once we get into the habit of gratitude, it becomes automatic in daily living.

Scripture:

> *This righteousness is given through faith in Jesus Christ to all who believe. There is no difference between Jew and Gentile, for all have sinned and fall short of the glory of God, and all are justified freely by his grace through the redemption that came by Christ Jesus.*
>
> Romans 3:22-24 (NIV)

> *But to each one of us grace has been given as Christ apportioned it.*
>
> Ephesians 4:7 (NIV)

For it is by grace you have been saved, through faith—
and this is not from yourselves, it is the gift of God—
not by works, so that no one can boast.

Ephesians 2:8-9 (NIV)

Grace and peace be yours in abundance through
the knowledge of God and of Jesus our Lord.

2 Peter 1:2 (NIV)

Experiences:

The teaching profession has changed and will continue to change. During these changes and challenging times, we learned to stay steadfast through prayer. One year, a second-grade teacher had a high teacher-student ratio, impacted by several needy and demanding students who made teaching in that classroom difficult despite the support. Contained therein were students who had emotional outbursts, discipline problems, strong-willed and resistant personalities that did not cooperate in any given way.

Do parents visit your classroom unannounced? How do you feel when this happens? Are you immediately on guard? When disciplining difficult students, parents visit the classroom and view the teacher as insensitive not understanding the dynamics of the classroom. Parents become belligerent and call the superintendent or principal. Teachers become discouraged with this type of behavior, feeling overwhelmed and contemplating leaving the district and the profession. This is often the result of feeling unsupported.

As colleagues, we encourage and listen to other teacher's distress, providing support and comfort while staying in faith through prayer. By grace we make it through times of turmoil, knowing the end of the school year is coming soon. Peace comes at the end of the year as the students move on to the next grade.

Confirmations:

- I am receiving the gift of special favor.
- I am shielded by grace and the light of the Lord.
- I am surrounded by God's love.

- I am a conqueror and will not be defeated.
- I am finding strategies and strength through faith and blessings.

Envision and Express the following:

- I see myself in control of my classroom.
- I see my students making progress despite all the obstacles.
- I accept the grace shining upon me.
- I envision blessings and rewards in my future.
- I perceive the light at the end of the tunnel.
- I view the end of the year approaching soon.
- My faith grows stronger every day.
- I believe in the gift of grace.
- The blessing of God will sustain me throughout the year.
- I believe and I have peace from the Lord.
- My guardian angels and my students' angels help us achieve in the classroom.

My desires are...

_____

_____

_____

_____

_____

_____

26
Humility

What is humility? It is the act or state of being humble and is not considered a weakness. It is strength that is under control with the quality of respect of others and a prerequisite to a spiritual man. Do you think teaching shows us how to be humble? Yes, we commit to serving our students with true humility, producing contentment and security. We receive grace and exaltation through our Lord Jesus Christ.

We lose sight of just how powerful we are as teachers. Children watch us all the time, as do other teachers and parents. In that event, we remind ourselves to be on our best behavior and be good role models. This is a tall order, but it eventually pays off.

Scripture:

> *Truly, I say to you, unless you turn and become like children, you will never enter the kingdom of heaven. Whoever humbles himself like this child is the greatest in the kingdom of heaven.*
> Matthew 18:3-4 (ESV)

> *Likewise, you who are younger, be subject to the elders. Clothe yourselves, all of you, with humility toward one another, for "God opposes the proud but gives grace to the humble." Humble yourselves, therefore, under the mighty hand of God so that at the proper time he may exalt you.*
> 1 Peter 5:5-6 (ESV)

He has told you, O man, what is good; and what does the Lord
require of you but to do justice, and to love kindness,
and to walk humbly with your God?

Micah 6:8 (ESV)

It is better to be humble in spirit with the lowly
than to divide the spoil with the proud.

Proverbs 16:19 (NASB)

Experiences:

Arrogance is the opposite of humility; therefore, it becomes a behavior of resistance. We are called instructors but truly, we only have one instructor, Christ. Have you met a person so resistant and full of pride that they do not listen to any other ideas? Occasionally in our profession, we encounter dissatisfied parents who do not fully understand and come to their own conclusion from what their child has told them, without hearing the teacher's side.

One time a frustrated student chose not to attend his reading intervention classes, as they were his lowest achieving area. He brought his grandparents to school saying the class was too easy and wanted out. Tests showed his performance low in reading comprehension skills. It became one excuse after another how to avoid the reading class. The student refused to read and resisted all attempts to complete his class work. The incident became blown out of proportion and well exaggerated.

With difficulty, we held a meeting with the grandparents to discuss an alternate way to meet this child's needs. Apparently, the grandson was out of control at home as well and the grandparents were at a loss. The conversation led to a change in our approach to serving the student that ultimately was successful for a short time. Although, later he became dissatisfied with the arrangement and a new set of problems emerged again.

Often the child lies about the class and the teacher. This happens frequently and we take a deep breath and humble ourselves. We rely on our documentation and record keeping, consoling angry parents to resolve the misunderstood circumstances.

Confirmations:

- I understand the spirit of humility.

- I am non-resistant.

- I listen for direction and instruction.

- I am exalted as I exercise humility.

- I practice the spirit of forgiveness and letting go.

- I am a winner and vindicated by my God.

Envision and Express the Following:

- I imagine myself humble and at peace.

- I feel my spirit strengthened.

- I see myself having good relationships with my students' parents.

- I view myself living justly and patiently.

- I see irritation leaving me.

- I see myself forming into a precious pearl.

- I receive the gift of grace and humbleness.

- My Lord is my comforter and redeemer.

- My voice speaks the truth with Jehovah's guidance.

- Justice will prevail in God's eye.

- I remind myself that I am the apple of His eye.

- God's hand is keeping me safe.

My desires are...

_____

_____

_____

_____

_____

27

Restoration

We are to live joyous lives without guilt and stay close in our communication with God through obedience. Christ does not want sin to separate us from Him. But by creating a strong relationship with Him, we more fully experience His love and peace. Forgiven are our crimson sins that are now as white as snow. He restores us in physical health, mental health, and spiritual health beyond and above what we were. Nothing is too hard! In prayer, we refine and align our spirit through faith in believing and receiving the gifts of God. We aim for restoration and healing, but it is all up to us when we allow and accept His grace.

Scripture:

Finally, brothers, rejoice. Aim for restoration,
comfort one another, agree with one another, live in peace;
and the God of love and peace will be with you.

2 Corinthians 13:11 (ESV)

Brothers if anyone is caught in any transgression, you who are
spiritual should restore him in a spirit of gentleness.
Keep watch on yourself, lest you too be tempted.

Galatians 6:1 (ESV)

Restore to me the joy of your salvation. Uphold me with a willing spirit.

Psalm 51:12 (WEB)

And that he may send Christ Jesus, who was ordained for you before,
whom heaven must receive until the times of restoration of all things,
which God spoke long ago by the mouth of his holy prophets.

Acts 3: 20-21 (WEB)

Experiences:

Little Johnny entered yet another new school after his parents went through a divorce and the dismantling of the home. Johnny ambled slowly down the hall with his head down feeling sad, alone, and defeated. Reluctantly, he stepped into the classroom feeling tense and self-conscience. Knowing his situation, the teacher made an attempt to make him feel welcome. How many students have you greeted in your classroom like Johnny? This scenario is common and reoccurring often in our schools.

Considering another experience, a family of four siblings lost a parent. The entire school felt the loss, for the parent was young and well known in our community. The children were devastated and it affected their school attendance and performance. This happened near the beginning of the school year. Remaining aware of the grieving process, the rest of the year was focused on providing normality in their daily lives. Restoration was slow and the inappropriate behavior of the children accentuated. We became more sympathetic and more accommodating to their needs with a spirit of gentleness and comfort for God brings beauty from ashes.

This change in life style can be devastating to parents and children. Children come to school brokenhearted and lose trust in everyone. This is apparent in their behavior and school performance. We, as teachers, since we work so closely with them, understand their pain and show compassion, care, and patience that further develop our own temperament. This is how we grow as teachers. Even the students, in time, through these changes, heal the wounds and restore their minds to a higher spiritual level. It is a learning experience for all.

Going through a difficult time such as losing friendships and dissolving relationships can be a heavy burden, and we suffer severe emotional losses. But, our Savior wants our mental health, lives, and souls renewed. The goal is to restore the close relationship with Him. When we allow

God to refresh us, our spirits are elevated to perfect harmony with the divine Creator.

Confirmations:

- I am strong and have a "can do" attitude.
- I am healthy and happy.
- I am gentle and comforting.
- I rejoice with aim of restoration.
- I am surrounded by love and compassion.

Envision and Express the Following:

- I see myself strong and energized.
- I envision myself healthy and whole.
- I see myself glowing with great color and physically fit.
- I view myself communicating with people in perfect balance.
- I see myself strong and full of confidence.
- I perceive myself restored in emotional and spiritual being.
- My wounded heart is restored and in peace.
- Thank you, Father, that I am restored back to a close relationship with you.
- I surrender to my Savior to carry me through this difficult time.
- I am fully recovered and restored.
- I forgive and I move forward with my life.

My desires are...

_____

_____

_____

_____

_____

28
God's Promises

When dealing with problems we must keep in mind God's promises that He is always faithful. The Bible is full of promises! It is important to know and use these in our lives and for our growth. We focus on the promises instead of the problems. God will only be in our lives to the extent of our invitation. Speak His promises first, have faith, and then trust the Lord to work on our behalf and to our advantage. The Holy Spirit is with us through adversities, as there is a purpose for these in our life.

How much trust do you have? When we trust in divine promises, we are transformed. God always keeps His promises of healing, peace, and heart satisfaction, deliverance from fear, overcoming temptations, and forgiveness. There are also promises of family, children, and marriage, protection, end of suffering, security, wisdom, and guidance. The Holy Spirit also takes care of all our needs such as food, shelter, clothing, job security, quality, and everlasting life. How strong is your faith? Through faith and believing, all can be attained. He has already delivered our needs and desires by always keeping His promises.

Scripture:

Be strong and courageous. Do not be afraid or terrified
because of them, for the Lord your God goes with you;
he will never leave you nor forsake you.

Deuteronomy 31:6 (NIV)

And we know that in all things God works for the good of those
who love him, who have been called according to his purpose.

Romans 8:28 (NIV)

Cast all your anxiety on him because he cares for you.

1 Peter 5:7 (NIV)

So do not fear, for I am with you; do not be dismayed,
for I am your God. I will strengthen you and help you;
I will uphold you with my righteous right hand.

Isaiah 41:10 (NIV)

Experiences:

We are encouraged knowing our Father never gives up on us. When we make mistakes, He is by our side. Every year during budget discussions, some teachers' positions were cut, putting everyone on pins and needles. We looked at what classes could be cut and possibly combine grade levels if the number of students did not materialize in the fall. This was not popular among the teachers or the parents.

Our librarian's position was on the chopping block every year. The whole faculty voted whether to retain the library/technology position. Throughout the years, the librarian had to pick up more duties and more demands on the job, with ordering technology and troubleshooting problems in all electronic devices. In addition to teaching library and technology classes full time, she had to teach and run the gifted and talented program because of limited budgets. She had to justify the importance of the position, which made her feel devalued and hung out on a limb all by herself. At times like this, we remind ourselves of the promises and stand firm, knowing He is still in control. Have faith and believe what is promised will come to pass.

Confirmations:

- I am good at my job and I will return next year.
- I walk strong and will soar high on the wings of eagles.
- I am an overcomer.

- I am faithful and fear no evil.
- I am thankful and take nothing for granted.

Envision and Express the Following:

- I visualize myself teaching a classroom full of students, in front of the whiteboard with a lesson plan in hand and Jesus standing beside me.
- I catch students in my classroom behaving well, focused, and ready to learn.
- I view myself healthy and living in abundance.
- I see myself in my car driving safely to school.
- I see my Creator strengthening and upholding me in His righteous right hand.
- God will never leave me nor forsake me.
- I believe in keeping His promises and I accept them.
- I exercise patience that what I desire will come to pass.
- I believe the Lord has supplied me with everything I need now.

My desires are...

_____

_____

_____

_____

_____

_____

In our district, we received many opportunities to increase our knowledge base and our salaries. We took advantage of these opportunities through professional development, step increases, and other means. Invest in yourself as much as you can early in your career and stay informed, believing you prosper.

Confirmations:
- I am receiving extra pay as my hard work is paying off.
- I am prosperous by the grace of Divine love.
- I am asking; therefore, through faith I receive.
- I am riding the waves in the ocean of abundance.
- I am sailing the winds of prosperity.
- I am climbing up the mountains of wealth and achievement.

Envision and Express the Following:
- I visualize my school in the top achieving category.
- I visualize my students at the top of their game.
- I see myself receiving a stipend for a high achieving school.
- I envision my students scoring high on the achievement tests.
- I see myself celebrating my accomplishments.
- My students are performing well on the exams.
- My salary is increasing and my bins are overflowing.
- My investments are multiplying.
- Our students are excelling.
- I sow; therefore, I reap.

My desires are...

_____

_____

_____

_____

30
Temptation

We are surrounded by temptations luring us to make choices every day. We seek the Lord to guide and reveal to us the right path to take. Be still and listen for the answer. The strength of the Lord will come and strengthen us. What are your temptations? With temptation, God will also provide the way of escape. "But I say, walk by the Spirit, and you will not gratify the desires of the flesh." Galatians 5:16 (ESV).

We guard ourselves from temptation by staying in the Word, for the flesh is weak. How can we overcome the temptation and wicked thoughts? Cancelling these thoughts helps us replace them with gratitude, compassion, love, and faith-filled words. This brings us closer into the brilliance of the enlightened world of the Holy Spirit.

Scripture:

Finally, be strong in the Lord and in the strength of his might. Put on the whole armor of God, that you may be able to stand against the schemes of the devil. For we do not wrestle against flesh and blood, but against the rulers, against the authorities, against the cosmic powers over this present darkness, against the spiritual forces of evil in the heavenly places.
Ephesians 6:10-12 (ESV)

And lead us not into temptation, but deliver us from evil.
Matthew 6:13 (ESV)

Do not be conformed to this world, but be transformed by the renewal of your mind, that by testing you may discern what is the will of God, what is good and acceptable and perfect.

Romans 12:2 (ESV)

Experiences:

When a student ran down the hall with his hands full, spilling candy as he passed by, the teacher knew something was up; this student had strong temptations of stealing and then not owning up to the deeds. Money, cell phones, candy, food, and nick-knacks disappeared from classrooms. We questioned the student and monitored all the cameras placed in the halls. Often, the student put the blame onto other students, causing many hours of interviews with the involved children.

Finally, after the time-consuming investigation, the student was identified. One-on-one consultations helped this student overcome temptation. Eventually, through hard work, the student's behavior slowly changed as he began to understand the implication of how his actions affected others. While working with the student, he was shown respect in a caring manner and how God's love transcends all.

We, as people of God, feel the urge to give in to our impulses because we let our guards down. Resisting temptations such as over indulging, lust, gluttony, or stealing can be difficult. We are inclined to give up when things become too intense. Then we ask the Holy Spirit for strength to overcome these temptations and get back to our purpose.

Confirmations:

- I am strong in the Lord.
- I am in control of my thoughts.
- I am renewing my mind with positive thoughts.
- I am believing God's hands are with me guiding me and keeping me from temptation.
- I am resisting the enemy's stronghold.

Envision and Express the Following:

- I see myself standing strong against temptations.
- I see my faith getting stronger and carrying me through.

- I imagine myself holding a sword and a shield and fighting the temptation with the word of God.
- I observe angels with their wings stretched out protecting me from temptations.
- "What then shall we say to these things? If God is for us, who can be against us?" Romans 8:31 (ESV)
- I can do all things through Christ.
- I will not be tempted because of my lack of self-control.
- I guard to resist temptation and serve Him only.
- I declare being sober-minded and firm in my faith to resist evil.

My desires are...

_____

_____

_____

_____

_____

_____

- I view myself forgiven and working toward forgiveness.
- I catch myself communicating clearly without condemnation.
- I see my heart full of the joy of the Lord.
- I forgive people who hurt me with false accusations.
- I let go of my anger and let Him carry it.
- If God is for me who can be against me?
- I must remember this is their thinking and not mine, and I will not hold onto it.
- I do not leave the door ajar for the enemy to come in to make accusations.
- I remind myself to be alert always.
- When appropriate I will remain silent, and let the Lord be my vindicator.
- No man shall prosper when they come against me.

My desires are...

_____

_____

_____

_____

_____

_____

32

Fruitfulness

God said live abundantly, be fruitful, and multiply on earth. Fruitful means the products of our lives, which can be good or bad. This is a result of whatever controls our hearts. A Christian is fruitful in the heart with the fruits of the Spirit. This affects our actions, activities, thoughts, and words with a desire to please and carry out His will. "But the fruit of the Spirit is love, joy, peace, patience, kindness, goodness, faithfulness, gentleness, self-control; against such things there is no law." Galatians 5:22-23 (ESV). We develop these character traits, as we become stronger in the Spirit. We can also endeavor to instill these in our students.

Scripture:

He will love you, bless you, and multiply you. He will also bless the fruit of your body and the fruit of your ground, your grain and your new wine and your oil, the increase of your livestock and the young of your flock, in the land which he swore to your fathers to give you.

Deuteronomy 7:13 (WEB)

Your wife shall be like a fruitful vine within your house; Your children like olive plants around your table.

Psalm 128:3 (NASB)

And He caused His people to be very fruitful, and made them stronger than their adversaries.

Psalm 105:24 (NASB)

For there will be peace for the seed; the vine will yield its fruit; the
land will yield its produce and the heavens will give their dew; and
I will cause the remnant of this people to inherit all these things.

Zechariah 8:12 (NASB)

Experiences:

When dealing with children with inappropriate behavioral issues, we exercise the fruits of the Spirit every day. We need to be mindful of the fruits of the Spirit, particularly with patience, gentleness, and self-control. When a student has a defiant personality and a strong will, it is best to keep the state of affairs under control without escalating it.

During the school year, we had a group of students with conduct problems who met every morning to address appropriate behavior. Some of the students would come to school angry from home, and this carried on for quite a while. In this class, the students discussed their feelings and addressed their needs for the day. The fruits of the Spirit were intertwined into this lesson using a feelings chart developed by the teacher. This chart started at the top with high good feelings, progressing down to low feelings. The students expressed their current feelings by indicating the level of emotion on the chart. A discussion of the possible causes commenced.

We further discussed possible ways to elevate oneself to a more positive emotional state of mind. This session was highly effective in helping students start the day with a positive attitude. These elevated feelings carried through the rest of the day.

Confirmations:
- I am calm and patient with my students.
- I am kind and gentle to everyone.
- I am fair and firm in my everyday life.
- I am in control of my thoughts and actions.
- I am loving, caring, and genuine in my character traits.
- I am at peace in my classroom and at home.

Envision and Express the Following:
- I see the child's attitude improving through God's grace.
- I visualize the state of affairs resolved.

- I perceive myself in control.
- I see help arriving as needed.
- I envision peace in my classroom and in my household.
- Kind words will come out of my mouth.
- My classroom is in control of their behavior.
- I give immediate feedback and positive reinforcement to my students.
- I deliver rewards and incentives for good behavior.
- I recognize inappropriate behavior and take appropriate steps to help my students.
- I stand by these without wavering. I believe and I receive!

My desires are...

_____

_____

_____

_____

_____

_____

33
Kindness

We are kind to each other, even to our enemies. We treat our students with kindness, for when kindness is given, kindness will return. God is forgiving, gracious, and compassionate. Like Him, we need to be slow to anger and abounding in love. Kindness becomes second nature in as much as we are strong in the Spirit.

Are you quick to anger? Then, train your mind to think kind thoughts and elevate your thinking, and view people as children of God beyond the physical appearance. What you sow, you will reap. Perform random acts of kindness. When you see someone in need of help, no matter where it is, offer to help. It takes a moment to spread kindness that will in turn spread to other people and will return to you.

Scripture:

Therefore, as God's chosen people, holy and dearly loved, clothe yourselves with compassion, kindness, humility, gentleness and patience.

Colossians 3:12 (NIV)

Now swear to me here before God that you will not deal falsely with me or my children or my descendants. Show to me and the country where you now reside as a foreigner the same kindness I have shown to you.

Genesis 21:23 (NIV)

May the Lord now show you kindness and faithfulness, and I too
will show you the same favor because you have done this.

2 Samuel 2:6 (NIV)

Praise the Lord, all you nations; extol him, all you peoples.
For great is his love toward us, and the faithfulness
of the Lord endures forever. Praise the Lord.

Psalm 117:1-2 (NIV)

Experiences:

Teachers perform kindness day in and day out for each other, their students, and the school community. We see the needs of our students. The students also observe teachers communicating with kindness and acceptance of other people. The children internalize the trait and implement it in their own lives.

It was November and the holidays were approaching. It was the season to model kindness and caring. During Thanksgiving and the winter season, we brought food and non-perishable items to give to our needy families. We also brought toys and clothes. We felt very strongly that we not only address the educational needs of our students but also their physical needs.

One student, when the family was presented with a packet of brand new clothes, spotted a pair of jeans and shoes. Knowing the clothes were intended for him put a big smile on his face and he jumped up and down with joy. His eyes welled up with tears, seeing the pair of jeans because they were always what he wanted. Kindness brings out the best in people and it enfolds us in the cloak of love. It does not take much to be kind to make someone else happy. We perform the act of kindness unconditionally whenever the occasion presents itself.

Confirmations:

- I am giving my time for service.
- I am wonderfully blessed; therefore, I can give to others.
- I am generous to all without finding fault.

- I am elevated in Spirit as I give to others.
- I am content to see joy in other people.

Envision and Express the Following:

- I see myself compassionate and of service to other people.
- I envision myself surrounded by grace and blessings.
- I see myself operating with love.
- I look at people with kindness.
- I view myself in the spirit of giving.
- Gentleness and kindness are mine.
- I do my job with a helpful and caring spirit.
- I am clothed with compassion.
- I will not lose sight of anyone who needs help.

My desires are...

_____

_____

_____

_____

_____

_____

34

Grieving

Grief is the natural reaction to any loss, be it death, health, employment, or the end of a relationship. Can we be at peace while we grieve? It is possible to be at peace in the mist of our suffering and keep moving forward without being stuck in grief for a long time? God gives us the grace and the blessings to get through difficult, trying times. Depression, feeling of guilt, anger, pain, denial, and sadness are natural feelings of loss. These emotions vary from person to person as they come in various phases of grief.

As we go through these stages, we can better accept the loss by understanding what is behind the feelings we experience. As a believer, turn to the Word for strength and comfort while going through the daily functions of life. If needed, seek professional help or the support of a family member to help you cope with the loss. Give yourself time, for with time the loss will ease your pain and you will be able to feel happiness again.

Scripture:

You, Lord, keep my lamp burning; my God turns my darkness into light.
Psalm 18:28 (NIV)

Have I not commanded you? Be strong and courageous.
Do not be afraid; do not be discouraged,
for the Lord your God will be with you wherever you go.
Joshua 1:9 (NIV)

My flesh and my heart may fail, but God is
the strength of my heart and my portion forever.
Psalm 73:26 (ESV)

Blessed are those who mourn, for they will be comforted.
Matthew 5:4 (NASB)

Experiences:

Experiencing the loss of a loved one brings heartache and pain that can be intense. Don't forget, the Lord comforts us and we are not left alone to suffer. This season of grieving shall pass with time. We ask God to remove the pain, sorrow, and grief from our hearts. Then we receive His healing, comfort, and peace, for the Lord understands our hurt and dries our tears. Lean on our Savior, believing He has a good plan for our future and will replace our pain with great joy.

A colleague went through severe loss of her young son in a car accident caused by speeding. This was followed by the loss of her mother and a few years later, the loss of her husband. The unbearable overwhelming grief kept this teacher in the dark and oppressed for a while. The staff supported and helped by taking turns bearing some of the load; thus, lighting the burden and being understanding of the circumstances.

Giving our time to listen and comfort our colleagues can be rewarding. There is a season for grieving and being in the dark. Then through faith with forgiveness, we slowly move to the light and the acceptance of the loss.

Confirmations:
- I am forgiven; therefore, I forgive.
- I accept loss, knowing my Savior will bring me out with great joy.
- I am strengthened and uplifted by His Word.
- I am hopeful that my grief shall also pass.
- I am strong and determined to persevere during this grieving time.

Envision and Express the Following:
- I see myself accepting the loss.
- I perceive myself strong and encouraged.

- I see myself breathing and alive.
- I envision my grieving heart healing.
- I see myself moving toward the light.
- Strength and vitality are mine.
- God is in control and I feel peace.
- Jesus is smiling on me.
- My loved ones are in heaven and I will one day see them again.
- When one door closes, another one opens.
- God has not forgotten me nor forsaken me.

My desires are...

_____

_____

_____

_____

_____

_____

35
Healing

When our hearts have grown dull, our ears can barely hear, our eyes have closed, our minds are cluttered and full of ill thoughts, what do we do? We look to the heavens for mercy. The prayer of faith will save the one who is sick, and our Redeemer will forgive the cluttered mind. Fill your mouth and mind with gracious words and your soul and the health of the body is restored.

When we are physically ill, we are emotionally broken as well. Speak His Word with the willingness to stay on course and believe in His power to heal. Utilize your faith to access the healing in a specific area of need. Find comfort through scripture with persistence and expect healing to occur. Stand firmly without wavering!

Scripture:

A joyful heart is good medicine, but a crushed spirit dries up the bones.
Proverbs 17:22 (ESV)

My son, be attentive to my words; incline your ear to my sayings. Let them not escape from your sight; keep them within your heart, for they are life to those who find them, and healing to all their flesh.
Proverbs 4:20-22 (ESV)

Fear not, for I am with you; be not dismayed, for I am your God; I will strengthen you, I will help you, I will uphold you with my righteous right hand.
Isaiah 41:10 (ESV)

And Peter said to him, "Aeneas, Jesus Christ heals you; rise and make your bed." And immediately he rose.

Acts 9:34 (ESV)

Experiences:

The healing of disease is possible through faith in prayer. We pray for healing and believe we are already healed through the Holy Spirit without wavering and without begging. We remind ourselves we serve a supernatural God who can do what science and medicine cannot. "Lord my God, I called to you for help, and you healed me." Psalm 30:2 (NIV). Take time to read healing scriptures daily, as this puts you in the state of mind for recovery. Be encouraged that the power of prayer heals and that He fulfills His promises.

We know teachers who went through difficult times with the diagnoses of cancer. The medical field helps as much as they can, but the rest is up to us to heal ourselves. We receive the gift of healing through our faith and our belief will make us whole and healthy again. Good health can become a reality through a forgiving heart. We are strong again through faith and meditation by thinking on healing verses.

We continually work on staying in balance through daily thanksgiving and in forgiveness of our enemies and ourselves. Forgiveness is one of the keys for faith to work. When we release forgiveness and anger, healing occurs. Friends, never take health for granted and stay on the path of righteousness.

Confirmations:

- I am balanced and centered.
- I am rested and rejuvenated.
- I am in excellent health.
- I eat well with a good appetite.
- I feel and look wonderful.
- I function well and have no fear.
- I soar on the thermal of the wind with my Lord, the Healer.

Envision and Express the Following:

- I see myself moving well.
- I see myself breathing well.
- I see myself sleeping well.
- I see myself healthy and fit.
- I see myself glowing and happy.
- My youth is renewed like an eagle.
- With His stripes, I am healed.
- The Holy Spirit has authority and dominion over my body, and I declare healing.
- God's steadfast love and mercy is healing me.
- My muscles are strong and serving me well.

My desires are...

_____

_____

_____

_____

_____

_____

36

Marriage

So God created mankind in his own image, in the image of God he created them; male and female he created them. God blessed them and said to them, "Be fruitful and increase in number; fill the earth and subdue it. Rule over the fish in the sea and the birds in the sky and over every living creature that moves on the ground.

Genesis 1:27-28 (NIV)

We all face ups and downs in marriage, and we can look to the Bible to remember the importance of the vows made to one another. We are careful of the words we speak as well as how we remind our spouses gingerly how they speak as well.

Instead of using hurtful words, use uplifting, praising words toward your spouse. A wife wants to feel loved by her husband and a husband wants to be respected by his wife. It is up to us to keep our house and family peaceful as the Lord has called us to live in peace. Be aware of the strength and power of marriage. For some people growing old with a spouse is easier than being alone. However, for others living alone and making the Heavenly Father the head of their household and the source of their being can be just as rewarding.

"Therefore, what God has joined together, let no one separate." Mark 10:9 (NIV). During marriage, remember the power of patience and forgiveness. It takes constant work to have a good marriage. Be aware of the tone of your voice, the expression on your face, and the body language when communicating with your spouse. Be kind to one another and forgive easily. Resist the temptation of the flesh, for the flesh is weak.

"Marriage should be honored by all, and the marriage bed kept pure, for God will judge the adulterer and all the sexually immoral." Hebrews 13:4 (NIV).

Scripture:

He who finds a wife finds what is good and receives favor from the Lord.
Proverbs 18:22 (NIV)

A wife of noble character who can find?
She is worth far more than rubies.
Proverbs 31:10 (NIV)

Always be humble and gentle. Be patient with each other, making allowance for each other's faults because of your love.
Make every effort to keep yourselves united in the Spirit,
binding yourselves together with peace.
Ephesians 4:2-3 (NLT)

Love is patient and kind; love does not envy or boast; it is not arrogant.
1 Corinthians 13:4 (ESV)

Experiences:

During troubling times, try to look at your spouse's strengths instead of their weaknesses. Do not focus on what is wrong; instead stop to listen for God's guidance. Every day we take the time to tell our spouses how much we love them, how important they are to us, and how proud we are of them. Tell them how handsome or how beautiful they are. Have a giving heart by surprising them with small gifts that can also lift their spirits.

Respect one another always, despite the disagreements, and be aware of the words that come out of your mouth. Trusting and building up your spouse brings respect to the relationship ergo, helping the marriage become a success. Always focus on what your spouse does well and know they are not perfect.

We knew a couple in which one of the spouses used hurtful and demeaning words that devalued the other person. This controlling behavior was very damaging and the marriage fell apart. Remember to hold your marriage in honor above all and always look for opportunities to say a word of encouragement.

Confirmations:

- I am in a strong and solid marriage.
- I celebrate the gift of marriage.
- I am thankful for God's gift of my spouse.
- I am grateful for a loving home.
- I am in a loving, respectful relationship.
- I am grateful for my family.

Envision and Express the Following:

- I appreciate us holding hands and working together.
- I see us in a loving embrace.
- I see a loving kiss bestowed upon me.
- I see us in prefect harmony with respect and honor.
- I perceive us making decisions about our family together.
- I see us agreeing how to handle problems.
- We give praises and worship in our home.
- We withstand all hardships together.
- I respect and make a good spouse.
- We are growing together through the Word.
- I focus on my spouse's strengths.
- Blessings and prosperity are ours.
- Our disagreements are resolved.
- Having a spouse is a good thing.

My desires are...

_____

_____

_____

37
Living Favor Minded

When we delight in and connect with our Divine Father, we open the door to His favor and grace. So, what is the key to living favor minded? The key to favor mindedness is faith and believing that gifts and favors are ours. We trust the Holy Spirit is going to show up at just the right time and turn a difficult situation around to our advantage. In return, preferential treatment is extended to us. This is the time when we express our gratitude by thanking the Lord for His favor.

To receive grace, we forgive and let go of anger. This keeps our heart pure and our mind clear of judgment to open the door of favor mindedness. One word of caution, do not take the favor of God for granted! When we are favor-minded, we develop confidence, a boldness that makes us stand out above all the rest.

Scripture:

Call to me, and I will answer you, and will show you great things, and difficult, which you don't know.
Jeremiah 33:3 (WEB)

Let us come boldly to the throne of our gracious God. There we will receive his mercy, and we will find grace to help us when we need it most.
Hebrews 4:16 (NLT)

Blessed be the God and Father of our Lord Jesus Christ, who has blessed us in Christ with every spiritual blessing in the heavenly places.
Ephesians 1:3 (ESV)

The grace of our Lord abounded exceedingly with faith and love which is in Christ Jesus.
1 Timothy 1:14 1(WEB)

Experiences:

There is no doubt we had the favor of God many times over the years of teaching. An example is how we both kept our jobs every year despite many reductions when the budget was limited. We thrived despite the many changing of hands in the administration, along with new procedures and guidelines. This happened over the course of twenty-one years in the same school of our liking and being close to home.

Another example of favor was when the district changed our school boundaries because the district built a new school nearby. Students attended the new school, causing our school population to decline. Our school fell into the low range of achievement and left us struggling to maintain and keep the school open.

How can you change the seemingly impossible? We went to work to market our school by passing out fliers, rearranging bus routes, promoting the curriculum, clubs, technology, library, music, and art. We also took time to pray by envisioning, expressing, and declaring the blessings of the Lord upon the school. Many prayers claimed the student population and achievement scores would increase to place us in a high performing category. In the end, with the grace of God, we acquired more students and made it into the high achieving zone in which our school flourished!

Confirmations:

- I am in the favor of God.
- I am obedient and I uphold His commandments.
- I am guided by the Holy Spirit and have a class that is learning and achieving.
- I am celebrated in heavenly places.
- I am humbled and ready to serve my school community.

Envision and Express the Following:

- I declare my school in the high-achieving range.
- I see myself highly favored.

- I view myself loved and cherished.
- I see myself respected and a highly-valued teacher.
- I observe myself surrounded by His grace.
- "Good morning, how are you?" I am a highly favored teacher and deeply honored thanks to our Lord!
- I have confidence in my wisdom and knowledge to impart to my students.
- I claim my intentions are for my students to achieve.
- I come boldly to the throne of grace.
- I acknowledge the grace of God is exceedingly abundant.
- I accept the mercy and the blessings of Christ.
- I will not operate or be threatened by fear.

My desires are...

_____

_____

_____

_____

_____

_____

38

Compassion

Teachers working with homeless, multicultural, and immigrant students from war-torn areas daily tend to develop a tender heart and empathy toward the students. These kids are shaped by us and we help them assimilate into our American society. We feel their pain and are concerned about their well-being. Practicing kindness daily becomes an integral aspect of our lives; otherwise, it can become dull and cold.

Compassion brings calmness to our central core. How can you measure compassion? No one can measure a teacher's compassion, selflessness, or how much they give to students aside from education. Our blessed Father has comforted us in all our afflictions so that we can comfort others in their discomfort and afflictions. Teachers are peacemakers emanating light that shines in darkness illumining generosity and love.

Scripture:

Blessed be the God and Father of our Lord Jesus Christ, the Father of mercies and God of all comfort, who comforts us in all our affliction, so that we may be able to comfort those who are in any affliction, with the comfort with which we ourselves are comforted by God.

2 Corinthians 1:3-4 (ESV)

Finally, all of you, have unity of mind, sympathy, brotherly love, a tender heart, and humble mind.

1 Peter 3:8 (ESV)

Blessed are the peacemakers, for they shall be called children of God.
Matthew 5:9 (NIV)

As each has received a gift, use it to serve one another, as good stewards of God's varied grace.
1 Peter 4:10 (ESV)

Light shines in the darkness for the godly. They are generous, compassionate, and righteous.
Psalm 112:4 (NLT)

Experiences:

Once we had a homeless family just out of a shelter that needed furniture and food supplies to get back on their feet. The children in that family had low self-esteem and lacked social and communication skills with adults and peers. One sibling walked around the school with his head down feeling defeated. The student had poor attendance that contributed to his lack of friends.

The other sibling exhibited angry behavior and acted aggressively toward his peers. Knowing the family crisis, the faculty was compelled to help them by donating furniture, clothing, and food. All the teachers helped the kids overcome the difficult time by giving additional attention and compassion to fill their needs. Eventually we could see the change in the students' demeanor and the improvement of academic skills. This has happened many times in our school when teachers came together to fill the gap.

Another time, a student came to us from a war-torn country and lived in a camp for a while. This student had a difficult time with social skills due to limited schooling. He had viewed and experienced war atrocities in his own country. Coming to America, the student spoke little English and had a difficult time communicating with teachers and peers.

When in school, the student would get up and walk out of the classroom and did not follow the ritual and routines of the classroom or the school. We had to teach the basics of communication and social interaction skills so he would fit in and assimilate in the culture of our community. Despite these limitations, it was obvious the student was intelligent and picked up English quickly, as he wanted to fit in with his peers.

During the year, we observed the change in this student's behavior. We were happy to see the accommodations put in place were beneficial. The student showed improvement through acquiring English by making gains in both academic and social skills.

Confirmations:

- I am thankful I can give love and compassion to needy students.
- I am grateful I live in America, the land of abundance.
- I am blessed and humbled to serve those in need.
- I am happy to make a difference in students' lives.
- I am sympathetic and kindhearted.

Envision and Express the Following:

- I envision my students happy and learning despite their difficulties.
- I see my students as well balanced, productive human beings contributing to their communities.
- I visualize comfort as I help others.
- I see myself as a servant to others with a loving heart.
- Kindness, mercy, and tender heartedness are mine.
- I let Christ rule my heart.
- The Lord gives me strength, courage, and well-being to be able to show acts of kindness and mercy.
- God has blessed me with all I need to comfort others.
- Divine love comes to me and I rejoice in a giving heart.

My desires are...

_____

_____

_____

_____

_____

_____

39

Making a Difference

Frequently, we are so busy teaching we forget that we are making a difference in our students' lives. Fear sets in, nothing we try works, and we tell ourselves we cannot do it anymore. But, we can pick ourselves up to endure and transform the lives of others. Teachers do make a difference through influencing and empowering students to find the purpose of their future. We do have the power within us to change the world!

During this process, we surrender and give God full control to handle what is best for us. We stay in peace knowing He makes it work for our benefit, as His plan for us can never be stopped. The Creator of the universe sees us as a masterpiece. We do not let anyone tear us down. We make a difference in molding our students' lives and our school community.

Scripture:

And let us not grow weary of doing good, for in due season we will reap, if we do not give up.
Galatians 6:9 (ESV)

Even so, let your light shine before men; that they may see your good works, and glorify your Father who is in heaven.
Matthew 5:16 (WEB)

Being confident of this very thing, that he who began a good work
in you will complete it until the day of Jesus Christ.

Philippians 1:6 (WEB)

For we are co-workers in God's service; you are
God's field, God's building.

1 Corinthians 3:9 (NIV)

Experiences:

We never know the impact we have on our students. One year, part of our writing curriculum required the students to write daily in their journals. This experience increased their written expression skills by improving their language and the grammar skills. In turn, their ideas became more developed. The most interesting pieces of writing were published into books that were on display and available for students to check out in the school library. Seeing the difference this made on a child's face when their book was published and on view for everyone to see was heartwarming. Students had big smiles and their self-esteem rose with a sense of accomplishment.

Consequently, years later a parent of a former student shared that the writing and publishing process influenced her child to go to college and major in English literature. Today, because of that early experience in writing, the student is a successful writer. The parent was appreciative of the difference this made in her child's life. The teacher felt a sense of accomplishment with a job well done.

Another example of making an impact in a student's life came at the end of the year. A parent showed gratitude by presenting the teacher with a thank you card and a small gift in appreciation for teaching her child how to read and write. The parent also expressed gratitude to this teacher for making a difference in improving her child's self-esteem. The student had difficulty with sound-symbol association and decoding unfamiliar words. The pupil also struggled with putting thoughts on paper and expressing ideas through writing. Eventually, the youngster came up to grade level and became an independent reader outperforming some of his classmates. Putting a spark in a child's heart to be successful makes a difference!

Confirmations:

- I am confident I am making a difference in my students' lives.

- I am inspired and I inspire others.

- I am strong and determined to make a difference.

- I am praising the Divine Father for the gift of teaching and changing the world.

- I am empowered by the Holy Spirit to make a difference in my students' success.

- I am uplifted doing good deeds.

Envision and Express the Following:

- I view myself as a co-worker in divine service.

- I see myself serving my students and encouraging them to do well.

- I see my light shine through my students.

- I envision my students and myself not giving up, for we are His masterpiece.

- I see God's plan working through me.

- It is His plan for me and can never be stopped.

- I have no fear that I can do it.

- I commit to helping others.

- I let the Holy Spirit be in control and He will always be by my side.

- I stay in peace with the spirit of gentleness and service.

- I stir myself and renew my thinking.

My desires are...

_____

_____

_____

_____

40
Gossip and Lies

Gossip and lies are hurtful and can destroy another person's reputation. If you do not see it, then do not speak of it. Spreading rumors can destroy your own life. How can you improve this attitude of gossip and lies? Learn to overlook other people's mistakes, avoid unnecessary babble, for it will lead people into more and more ungodliness. If you are not part of the problem or solution, change the subject or close your mouth. If you are a gossiper, ask God to help you with this weakness. Learn to stay silent in difficult situations. Guard your mouth; otherwise, you are open to join the gossip. Therefore, you are opening the door for calamity to come into your own life.

Scripture:

Let no corrupting talk come out of your mouths, but only such as is good for building up, as fits the occasion, that it may give grace to those who hear.
Ephesians 4:29 (ESV)

A dishonest man spread strife, and a whisperer separates close friends.
Proverbs 16:28 (ESV)

To speak evil of no one, to avoid quarreling, to be gentle, and to show perfect courtesy toward all people.
Titus 3:2 (ESV)

Hide me from the secret plots of the wicked, from the throng of evildoers, who whet their tongues like swords, who aim bitter words like arrows, shooting from ambush at the blameless, shooting at him suddenly and without fear.

Psalm 64:2-4 (ESV)

You shall not go around as a slanderer among your people, and you shall not stand up against the life of your neighbor: I am Lord.

Leviticus 19:16 (ESV)

Experiences:

Working in a school with hundreds of people puts you in a position where you must sift out unnecessary and excessive talk. Stay professional and focus on your students. When you know a person is known to gossip, stay away and do not associate yourself with that person. When you find yourself in a gathering hearing unnecessary information, be quick to remove yourself from that group.

Once, an event occurred in which a parent came to pick up their child from our school at the end of the day. The police were notified that this parent was going to be at our school at this specific time. The police wanted to apprehend this parent on an issue that had nothing to do with the school.

Meanwhile having heard this, a staff member spread a rumor that they were there to pick up another teacher because they thought it was cute and funny. People were concerned, and the teacher was hurt from the gossip and false accusations. As a result, the principal called a faculty meeting to clarify the rumors. The gossiping teacher was reprimanded and asked to apologize for irresponsible and unprofessional conduct. Putting fear in teachers' hearts is never ok. The principal handled the situation firmly and immediately.

Confirmations:
- I keep quiet and guard my mouth always.
- I am free of all past hurts.
- I am strong in the Lord.

- I am developing a strong spirit.
- I do not repeat words of slander, gossip, and malice.
- I do not take any part in jokes that hurt.

Envision and Express the Following:

- I perceive myself as trustworthy in spirit.
- I see myself free of false condemnations.
- I view myself at peace and forgiving my enemies.
- I catch myself showing courtesy to people.
- I look upon people without judgment.
- I speak evil of no one.
- I guard my ears from the babble talk.
- I do not repeat or listen to angry talk.
- My faith is strong in love.
- I give people the benefit of the doubt.
- I forgive people when they make mistakes.

My desires are...

_____

_____

_____

_____

_____

_____

41

Fear and Anxiety

Everyone at some time has feelings of fear and anxiety and we become impatient and anxious. When we allow fear to take root we do not think clearly and are not productive. We become overwhelmed when we have due dates looming, report cards, testing, parent-teacher conferences, evaluations, and accountability.

How do we handle fear? When we feel anxious: Stop, take a deep breath, and come into the presence of God by prioritizing a "to do" list to accomplish. Complete one task at a time, checking it off the list for He has given us the grace of love, power, and self-discipline. Remember also to go into prayer and meditation to align your being with the Holy Spirit.

Scripture:

Be strong and courageous. Do not fear or be in dread of them, for it is the Lord your God who goes with you. He will not leave you or forsake you.

Deuteronomy 31:6 (ESV)

Fear not, for I am with you; be not dismayed, for I am your God; I will strengthen you, I will help you, I will uphold you with my righteous right hand.

Isaiah 41:10 (ESV)

When I am afraid, I put my trust in you. In God, whose
word I praise—in God I trust and am not afraid.
What can mere mortals do to me?

Psalm 56:3-4 (NIV)

Therefore I tell you, do not be anxious about your life,
what you will eat or what you will drink, nor about your body,
what you will put on. Is not the life more than food, and the body
more than clothing? Look at the birds of the air: they neither sow
nor reap nor gather into the barns, and yet your heavenly Father
feeds them. Are you not of more value than they?

Matthew 6:25-26 (ESV)

Experiences:

There are many urgent deadlines during the year, but we stay focused on our students and keep their best interests at heart. The students also get anxious as we press our demands on them. Instilling fear is not productive, but is often done to teachers, and unfortunately, it filters down to the students through excessive testing, test score expectations, and data reports on all students. Teacher evaluations have become brutal with almost daily observations that include precise prescribed language deliverance and format.

On one observation, a teacher was marked down for not stating the precise language during a lesson with preschoolers. The proposed words to be used by the teacher were not stated in the evaluation manual but were expected to be used even though the student's age did not allow them to comprehend this vocabulary. The age gap of maturity is varied and even a month or two at this age makes a big difference. When observed, this age variability is noticeable in student behaviors and skill acquisitions. Such precise evaluations hinder our spontaneity and productivity. As teachers, these practices make us feel incompetent and fearful doubting our expertise. As believers, we work through the fear and anxiety and stay focused on God's comforting words.

Confirmations:

- I am fully creative and a distinguished teacher.
- I am the head and not the tail.

- I am organized and meet all the deadlines.
- I am strengthened by the Word of God, and He will uphold me with His righteous right hand.
- I am the top and not the bottom.

Envision and Express the Following:

- I view myself as an excellent teacher.
- I perceive myself as a rising star.
- I see myself organized and happy in the teaching profession.
- I see my students full of enthusiasm and ready to learn.
- I see no fear looming over my head.
- I put my trust in the Lord.
- I fear not for God is with me.
- I am full of thanksgiving and the peace of God.
- My heart and mind are guarded through Christ Jesus.
- My fear and anxiety is diminished.
- I have accomplished my tasks.

My desires are...

_____

_____

_____

_____

_____

_____

42
Tolerance

Tolerance in the work place is to keep an open mind to accept other people's opinions and behavior to a point. It is also necessary to be understanding, yet there are behaviors that are intolerable. To what extent are you tolerant of people? Are you quick to anger? Patience and forgiveness of other people's mistakes and weaknesses can turn into a more positive experience for all.

There are times we agree to disagree as we work together. We also focus on things we have in common to successfully resolve problems; inasmuch as, we also appreciate the tolerance of others. Keeping the peace brings joy and happiness. However, there is no tolerance for evil intentions, misconduct or corruption. As children of God we are expected to behave accordingly to benefit all and to pass the spirit of tolerance onto our students.

Scripture:

I appeal to you, brothers, to watch out for those who cause divisions and create obstacles contrary to the doctrine that you have been taught; avoid them.
Romans 16:17 (ESV)

With all humility and gentleness, with patience, bearing with one another in love.
Ephesians 4:2 (ESV)

Gracious words are like a honeycomb, sweetness to the
soul and health to the body.

Proverbs 16:24 (ESV)

If anyone hears my words and does not keep them, I do not judge
him; for I did not come to judge the world but to save the world.

John 12:47 (ESV)

There is neither Jew nor Gentile, neither slave nor free, nor is there
male or female, for you are all one in Christ Jesus.

Galatians 3:28 (NIV)

Experiences:

We are all valuable and bring our own knowledge and understanding to the table. Tolerance and leniency of other people's opinion as well as benevolence should be considered. Do you know someone who dominates or controls conversations? We all know someone who overstates their opinion to make a point trying to dominate and maneuver others to their way of thinking. The controlling personality takes over at meetings and others feel intimidated in expressing their thoughts, which leads to silence.

The faculty was asked to participate in a new program having teachers visit students and parents in their environment. After much discussion, we were asked to vote whether or not we were on board for this program. Teachers with dominating personalities persuaded the faculty to adopt the new program to benefit the school community. The idea was to discuss with the parents their child's hopes, dreams, and where they see their child in ten years. Some parents tried to avoid us in visiting their homes because they were working parents and their time was limited.

It was mandated we visit three families or more in pairs to fulfill the requirement of the program. Since parents and teachers were busy, it was difficult to arrange appropriate times to meet. In the end, the parents were reluctant to meet and it all fell on the teacher's shoulders to push for meetings to make this program a success. Overall, it was stressful on the parents as well as the teachers.

There were many such occasions in which teachers had to be open-minded of the programs and policies that we were instructed to carry out. Often, we had no choice but to go with the flow and accept the change. We were expected whether we agreed or disagreed to make it a success. As a result, being tolerant avoids creating division and obstacles among the staff for the sake of the students and school success.

Confirmations:

- I maintain the unity of the Spirit in the bond of peace.
- I am complete in my joy by being of the same mind as my colleagues.
- I am open-minded of decisions made.
- I am tolerant of dominating personalities.
- I am at peace to make the program happen.

Envision and Express the Following:

- I visualize myself as a peacemaker.
- I see unity among the staff.
- I view the new program being successful for the good of the whole.
- I visualize parents' cooperation.
- I envision God's kindness coming through me.
- I cause no division within the faculty.
- I do not create unnecessary obstacles against protocol.
- I do nothing from rivalry or conceit but in humility.
- I look not only to my own interests but also to the interests of others.
- I will not be tolerant of unacceptable behavior or intention.

My desires are...

_____

_____

_____

_____

_____

_____

43

Depression

Depression is an emotional feeling we experience from time to time. It can be severe for some people, but we can interrupt the depressed thinking by bringing ourselves out of the darkness and into the light. We are responsible for our own happiness. We are not responsible for another person's happiness. How we handle circumstances make a difference in our state of mind. We do have the power to uplift and renew our minds. When we are down the enemy creeps in and creates multiple problems.

What are ways to bring ourselves out of depression? One remedy to come out of the darkness is to provide service to other people and use encouraging words and scriptures by meditating. Other ways to lift our mood is getting out into the sunlight every day, taking walks, enjoying the outdoors, and listening to uplifting music. Give yourself some time to feel better and your life to get healthier. Meanwhile, stay close for guidance and know that God loves and values us as He has an amazing future for us.

Scripture:

It is the Lord who goes before you. He will be with you;
he will not leave you or forsake you. Do not fear or be dismayed.
Deuteronomy 31:8 (ESV)

The righteous cry out, and the Lord hears them;
he delivers them from all their troubles.
Psalm 34:17 (NIV)

Praise be to the God and Father of our Lord Jesus Christ, the Father of compassion and the God of all comfort, who comforts us in all our troubles, so that we can comfort those in any trouble with comfort we ourselves receive from God.

2 Corinthians 1:3-4 (NIV)

Do not conform to the pattern of this world, but be transformed by the renewing of your mind. Then you will be able to test and approve what God's will is—his good, pleasing and perfect will.

Romans 12:2 (NIV)

Experiences:

Depression is when we lose hope and see no way out. When expectations are not met discouragement and self-loathing become apparent. We may not be able to bring ourselves out of depression alone, and it is wise to seek professional help and support. It might become necessary to receive medication and medical help to put your body in balance.

We know teachers who become depressed. On one occasion, one of our colleagues went through a deep depression because of health and relationship problems. She became disheartened and found it difficult to fulfill the expectations of the job. This teacher had taught for many years but was placed on a plan of improvement. Our friend felt alone with a fear of abandonment.

The severe depression brought on other health problems that led to a stroke. In addition, a few of us rallied around our colleague with prayer sessions, supporting and uplifting her with hope that things would get better. We helped this teacher by giving her permission to grieve and forgive herself. We encouraged her to reach deep inside for faith that God will intervene and fight the battle for her. Our dear friend passed away from a heart attack brought on by depression and a broken heart. The death affected the whole school community and left us feeling empty and sad.

Confirmation:

- I am beautiful inside and out.

- I am enough and more.

- I am surrounded by the love of God.
- I am well able to overcome with God's help.
- I am delivered from all my troubles.
- I am grateful for every breath I take and from the comfort of the Creator.
- I am grateful for the support of friends and family.

Envision and Express the Following:

- I see myself finishing the school year in a positive note.
- I see myself peaceful in my happy place.
- I envision myself conquering the condition.
- I visualize myself recovering and coming out better than before.
- I see myself happy and productive again.
- My soul is healing.
- Everything is getting better every day, and I praise the Lord.
- I give thanks for God shielding me and helping me lift my head high.
- I claim happiness and recovery through this season.
- This shall pass and my heart will be renewed.

My desires are...

_____

_____

_____

_____

_____

_____

44

Rest and Sleep

It is important for us to rest and rejuvenate our mind and bodies. Are you lacking sleep? Quality sleep helps maintain good health and well-being, as well as protects us from illnesses. Sleep opens the door for the Holy Spirit to communicate with us through dreams and visions by giving us warnings of events to come. We found these revealing dreams always true yet, some people can have deep intuitions that are just as revealing.

There are times when stress mounts up, and we have trouble getting to a relaxed state of mind. Replaying the events of the day creates a barrier of fear that robs us of our sleep. How can we stop this pattern? The solution is to release it and change our thinking to more relaxed thoughts. Also, sometimes what we eat disrupts our sleep pattern. We can transform ourselves to a restful place where we are calm and at peace. Close your eyes, let go, trust, and think of nothing, for you have God's blessings.

Scripture:

When you lie down, you will not be afraid;
when you lie down, your sleep will be sweet.

Proverbs 3:24 (NIV)

I laid myself down and slept. I awakened; for Yahweh sustains me.

Psalm 3:5 (WEB)

In peace I will both lay myself down and sleep, for you,
Yahweh alone, make me live in safety.
Psalm 4:8 (WEB)

At this I awoke and looked, and my sleep was pleasant to me.
Jeremiah 31:26 (ESV)

Experiences:

Sleep is necessary for our health and well-being so that we can do our best in serving our students. We know teachers who came to school saying they could not sleep because of mounting deadlines and their heavy amount of work. Processing all the coming events at school can leave us numb and anxious. The increased number of tests given to students and the preparation for these tests is time consuming.

We see teachers drag themselves to school with bags under their eyes from exhaustion and lack of sleep. But, we let go of our troubles and put our trust in God. We are confident of our talents and abilities. The rules and regulations of setting up the tests can impact our rest, but only if we allow it. We let go of the fear, be in the now, and take one day at a time. Rest assured you are doing everything possible and know your students best.

On the other hand, we had teachers who shared with us their profound dreams warning them of upcoming difficult incidences. These proved to be vital in preparation and making wise choices when the incidences became a reality. One teacher always saw a snake in her room that warned her there is an enemy lurking around. This was a warning of caution to be careful and be alert. This proved to be true as trouble developed.

Another dream warned us of an upcoming unrest among the faculty. The teacher saw a ship on troubled waters during a fierce storm and the two of us were observing the ship from the shore. This dream proved to be true, for trouble did happen in our school and prepared us not to be a part of the unrest. These profound dreams always manifested themselves into reality. For this reason, do not take for granted the dreams and visions you experience for God always has your best interests at heart.

Confirmations:

- I am relaxed and rested.
- I am at peace and ready for rest.
- I am perfectly healthy in mind, body, and spirit.
- I am grateful for my sleep.
- I am feeling refreshed and I fear no evil.
- I am calm and sleeping well.

Envision and Express the Following:

- I visualize my head on my pillow resting peacefully.
- I view my body relaxed and sleeping.
- I see myself comfortable in my bed.
- I perceive myself rested and rejuvenated in the morning.
- I see myself sleeping throughout the night.
- I have a restful night.
- I declare pleasant dreams.
- Come morning I feel refreshed.
- My youth is renewed like an eagle.
- My thoughts are clear and not cluttered.
- I claim sweet sleep.
- My Lord sustains me.

My desires are...

_____

_____

_____

_____

_____

_____

45
Disabilities

We have students with varied degrees of disabilities in our schools. It is not easy dealing with children with disabilities; however, they are our responsibility and we are accountable for their educational growth. Some of these kids are stronger, braver, and occasionally more compassionate than the rest. Our Lord has an unconditional love for all despite our disabilities. "He has created us anew in Christ Jesus so we can do the good things he planned for us long ago." Ephesians 2:10 (NLT). Every child is important and there is a purpose to help us love and grow from each other through patience and acceptance of their individual needs.

Scripture:

*See that you do not despise one of these little ones.
For I tell you that in heaven their angels always see
the face of my Father who is in heaven.*
Matthew 18:10 (ESV)

*For no one who has a blemish shall draw near, a man blind or
lame, or one who has a mutilated face or a limb too long.*
Leviticus 21:18 (ESV)

*But God, being rich in mercy, because of His great love
with which He loved us.*
Ephesians 2:4 (NASB)

Than a demon-possessed man who was blind and mute
was brought to Jesus, and He healed him,
so that the mute man spoke and saw.
Matthew 12:22 (NASB)

He who mocks the poor taunts his Maker;
He who rejoices at calamity will not go unpunished.
Proverbs 17:5 (NASB)

Experiences:

Special education teachers work cooperatively with regular classroom teachers with the inclusion of the special needs students in general education. Occasionally, general education teachers have the attitude of not wanting the special needs students in their classrooms. This makes the special education teachers feel even stronger to vouch for their special needs students. Whether we like it or not we have to accept and teach these young minds. We need to increase our patience, tolerance, and stand by their side.

Students with disabilities need a sense of belonging and someone to advocate for them. Special education teachers work with these students to teach them strategies and collaborate with classroom teachers to close the educational gap. A teacher had a student who could not read despite everyone's efforts. The child had good language skills and therefore could carry on a conversation with peers and adults. This pupil was very sweet, well behaved, and well accepted by everyone.

Using a technological program, due to the lack of writing ability, this student could verbalize thoughts by voice recording using the computer to complete and print written reports. This brought a big smile on the face of the child feeling invigorated and motivated to pursue further academic skills. Classroom teachers became more tolerant of this kid because they observed the progress made. Eventually, the student became successful in school with adult assistance.

Confirmations:

- I am compassionate and patient.
- I am tolerant and accepting of all students.

- I am grateful for the opportunity to work with students with disabilities.
- I am expanding my horizon through working with these students.
- I am learning and growing through my special need students.

Envision and Express the Following:

- I visualize my students staying on task and improving their skills.
- I see myself open and receptive to new ideas.
- I perceive my attitude and behavior changing positively toward these students.
- I see them as an asset instead of a hindrance to my classroom.
- I see myself receiving help and guidance as needed.
- Things happen for good reasons.
- I pray for boosts of energy to sustain me throughout the year.
- Help is coming from different sources.
- I believe and I receive the favor of God.
- I accept the mercy bestowed upon me.
- I wish for blessings and grace to come to all my students.
- The angels assigned to me and my students are working on our behalf.

My desires are...

_____

_____

_____

_____

_____

_____

46
Anger and Bitterness

How does holding on to anger affect our lives? Anger can get us into deep trouble, and holding onto anger leads us to bitterness. It keeps us from experiencing the good and wonderful things in store for us. If not handled properly, we end up paying the consequences such as illness, accidents, or depression. When anger and bitterness enter our life, we shift our focus from light to darkness.

When anger is manifested through the stress of work, relationships, or family, we deal with it so it does not become part of our personality. How can we release our anger? We release our anger by having faith to lighten our burden. If not handled well, holding on to anger and getting caught up in it keeps us from moving forward preventing a happy, successful life. Remember, we are not victims but are victors through forgiveness.

Scripture:

For pressing milk produces curds, pressing the nose produces blood,
and pressing anger produces strife.

Proverbs 30:33 (ESV)

Don't be hasty in your spirit to be angry,
or anger rests in the bosom of fools.

Ecclesiastes 7:9 (WEB)

A hot-tempered man stirs up strife, but he who is slow to anger
quiets contention.

Proverbs 15:18 (ESV)

Refrain from anger, and forsake wrath!
Fret not yourself; it tends only to evil.

Psalm 37:8 (ESV)

Experiences:

Working in a building with a large population of students and adults, we are bound to have disagreements and feel angry at times. Anger is not a sin but alerts us to something that is not right. There was a time a meeting was held without the librarian's presence. The librarian was out of town attending family funerals and emergencies. Key decisions were made concerning the library without important knowledge or input from the librarian.

It was decided that the librarian would not be involved in student book checkout. This affected the knowledge of what students chose to read for pleasure, not meeting their needs and limiting the knowledge of ordering high interest books. The librarian was expected to strictly teach classes. The decision did not set well with the librarian and some of the teachers. This brought out anger and distrust of the procedure.

To disperse the anger, it was crucial to receive guidance and comfort from God, staying still and listening for revelation. Dealing with the problem immediately through proper communication and expressing strong feelings made a difference. However, the anger was not allowed to turn into bitterness through the acceptance of the final decision having the teachers check out their own children's books. In due time, the process of letting go of the anger was achieved through forgiveness.

Confirmations:

- I am confident that God works on my behalf.
- I am letting go of the anger through expressing my feelings.
- I am calm during difficulties.

- I am divinely blessed as I start my day.
- I am in control of my anger and distress.
- I am creative and productive.
- I am happy and I am a blessing to others.

Envision and Express the Following:

- I declare myself a conqueror.
- I catch myself not responding to anger so quickly.
- I remind myself to listen before I speak.
- I see myself understanding and not judging people.
- I envision myself forgiving instead of holding onto anger.
- I thank His Holiness for my wisdom that comes from the Lord.
- My decisions are based on the Word.
- I let go and let God be in control.
- My emotions are calm.

My desires are...

_____

_____

_____

_____

_____

_____

47

Peace and Quiet

Peace and quiet are hard to attain, and it takes work to get there in a noisy world. If we want tranquility, be still and listen so it seeps into your deepest core. We put our trust and worries in God's hands. Our joy comes from above, not from man, for fear from man takes our serenity away.

When there is turmoil and strife battling in our heads, we go to a quiet place to meditate without interruptions and take deep breaths to relax our minds and experience peace. The Holy One is our strength and our joy and gives our burdened heart rest and harmony, for He is always welcomed in our midst. It is up to us to quiet our minds and listen, for God always has a word of comfort to share.

Scripture:

The Lord gives strength to his people;
the Lord blesses his people with peace.

Psalm 29:11 (NIV)

You will go out in joy and be led forth in peace;
the mountains and hills will burst into song before you,
and all the trees of the field will clap their hands.

Isaiah 55:12 (NIV)

Come to me, all you who are weary and burdened, and I will
give you rest. Take my yoke upon you and learn from me, for I am
gentle and humble in heart, and you will find rest for your souls.
For my yoke is easy and my burden is light.

Matthew 11:28-30 (NIV)

Peace I leave with you; my peace I give you.
I do not give to you as the world gives.
Do not let your hearts be troubled and do not be afraid.

John 14:27 (NIV)

Experiences:

It was important for us during our busy schedule to close the door and turn off the lights during planning or at lunch. We came together frustrated, anxious, and ready to vent, as demands were ever so present. Do you have someone you can trust to vent to without fear? We all need someone like that. It is vital to release anger and frustrations quickly instead of revisiting them over and over in our minds.

Frequently, we helped each other to look at trouble from a different perspective. For example, one time in the middle of teaching, an administrator came into our room unexpectedly. The administer requested that a task be performed, requiring many hours of completing forms and contacting parents and affiliated teachers for a meeting about a student's lack of progress and behavior. In this moment, we had to take a step back, shift gears, and look at the request from a different perspective, realizing the task had to be done. It took some reprioritizing of tasks at hand to organize the meeting. We prompted ourselves to put our worries in God's hands to pull us out of excessive complaining.

To rise above, we closed our eyes and performed slow breathing techniques to quiet our minds and meditate without guilt. We also prayed and wrote confirmations in our journals to obtain tranquility and peace. This forced us to retreat and find ourselves. The rest of the day went much smoother, and we could cope with whatever came our way.

Confirmations:

- I am quiet with a sense of calmness
- I am rested with a clear mind.
- I am at peace always in every way.
- I am thankful for a sound mind.
- I am grateful that I am safe in God's love.
- I am grateful I have a friend to vent to.
- I am thankful for God's grace that I can handle unexpected events.

Envision and Express the Following:

- I view myself with light burdens.
- I see myself managing my day with ease.
- I envision myself rested and taking on challenges with a peaceful heart.
- I see myself taking the time to meditate during my break.
- I visualize myself completing the task with success.
- I rest my active mind.
- My heart is not troubled or afraid.
- Peace and grace are upon me.
- I take the time during my day to praise the Lord.
- I receive God's mercy and blessings.

My desires are...

_____

_____

_____

_____

_____

48
Freedom

What does freedom mean to you? Freedom is the ability to express our thoughts without ridicule or fear of repercussion. The spirit of exercising love and self-control is freedom. Teachers often feel they have no freedom due to prescribed curriculum, the fidelity of programs, and time restraints. A feeling of powerlessness and lack of control dampens our enthusiasm.

One way of claiming our freedom is memorizing and learning verses about freedom. Through reciting these verses, we acquire freedom of spirit. In approaching the Lord through our faith with renewed confidence, we release the control. We do not have to worry, for God holds fear at bay and helps us find our peace.

Scripture:

For God didn't give us a spirit of fear,
but of power, love, and self-control.
2 Timothy 1:7 (WEB)

And you will know the truth, and the truth will set you free.
John 8:32 (ESV)

Now the Lord is the Spirit, and where the Spirit of the Lord is,
there is freedom.
2 Corinthians 3:17 (NIV)

For you were called to freedom, brothers.
Only do not use your freedom as an opportunity for the flesh,
but through love serve one another.

Galatians 5:13 (ESV)

Experiences:

Several years ago, we had a math program in which teachers were imposed to teach certain concepts with rigid pacing of the curriculum each day. Lesson plans had to be ready and precise on the teacher's desk, reflecting what was taught in the classroom. Frequent teacher observations made sure the teacher was on target. Furthermore, coaches came to observe the teachers to assure the lessons were rigorous and teachers were keeping up with the protocol of the math program. Teachers were in panic mode when noticing coaches entering their classrooms; knowing they were behind in keeping up with the timing of lessons.

Lesson plans were checked and when teachers were behind they were given advice how to accelerate the content on a timely manner. Everybody had to be on the same content, same page at a certain time of the day to keep the fidelity of the program. It was unbelievable to comprehend how rigid the program was, bringing much fear in everyone's heart. Nevertheless, the curriculum was completed with much confusion and frustration because it did not make sense. With this fast-regimented pacing, the students did not grasp the content. The teachers felt restricted in the freedom and trust to do what is best for their students.

Confirmations:

- I am in control of my thoughts.
- I am free of frustration.
- I am strong in my faith.
- I am quiet and productive in all I do.
- I am an accomplished teacher.

Envision and Express the Following:

- I visualize myself as a successful teacher.
- I see myself competent to teach any curriculum.

- I envision myself making wise choices and in control.
- I see myself cooperating and collaborating with my colleagues.
- I see myself keeping the fidelity of the Holy Spirit.
- I walk with the Spirit of the Lord.
- In God's timing, I can do all things through Christ.
- I declare I have the ability and wisdom to teach appropriately.
- I have patience and self-confidence.
- I am a team player.

My desires are...

_____

_____

_____

_____

_____

_____

49
Diet and Dieting

Nervousness and stress bring about the habit of overeating, and gluttony is often overlooked in our society. Proper exercise to balance our bodies and minds is important, yet difficult to find the time to take care of ourselves. Over indulgence leads to health problems and our well-being.

Temperance is the key! We all enjoy food. Exercising self-control and managing the size portion of our intake of foods is essential. God gave us our bodies as temples of the Holy Spirit, and we need to be mindful of what goes in our mouths. We eat and drink in the glory of the Father, for He gives us all we need to satisfy our hunger. Food is fuel for our bodies to help us perform and serve justly one another.

Scripture:

Or do you not know that your body is a temple of the Holy Spirit within you, whom you have from God? You are not your own, for you were bought with a price. So glorify God in your body.

1 Corinthians 6:19-20 (ESV)

Jesus said to them, "I am the bread of life; whoever comes to me shall not hunger, and whoever believes in me shall never thirst."

John 6:35 (ESV)

Do you not know that you are God's temple
and that God's Spirit dwells in you?

1 Corinthians 3:16 (ESV)

Then God said, "Behold, I have given you every plant yielding seed
that is on the surface of all the earth, and every tree
which has fruit yielding seed; it shall be food for you."

Genesis 1:29 (NASB)

So whether you eat or drink or whatever you do,
do it all to the glory of God.

1 Corinthians 10:31(NIV)

Experiences:

The teacher's lounge is always full of food. Food is always around us, but it is up to us to have self-control and make good choices. Being overweight is a health concern, slows us down, and keeps us from performing our best. We knew teachers with health problems. They had trouble staying alert and being able to move efficiently and promptly to keep up with the students' activity.

Health concerns are a possibility through stress and fear, but asking God to help us curb our appetite and gain control of our food habits can help us lose to a healthy weight. The health concern can be subsided through careful food choices, portions, and exercise. Moving and keeping active is critical to maintaining a healthy body. Just remember to eat half and move more! We had this problem, as we both were pre-diabetic. We each lost twenty pounds by keeping close track of our calorie intake and the diabetic symptoms subsided.

Another strategy we did to lose weight was to make a list of confirmations, put them on our mirrors and read them every morning, as we got dressed. We continue today to keep a close eye on our health and our food selections through prayer and meditation. It is constant and an on-going battle, yet we need to take care of ourselves. It can be achieved!

Confirmations:

- I am at a healthy weight.
- I am full and satisfied.
- I am thin and slender.
- I am perfectly healthy in mind, body, and spirit.
- I am losing weight through God's help.
- I don't overeat, and I make good healthy food choices.

Envision and Express the Following:

- I visualize myself looking attractive and slender.
- I imagine myself in a fitting slim pair of jeans.
- I catch myself choosing food wisely.
- I see myself at a perfect weight.
- I perceive myself more active.
- I lose weight quickly and effortlessly.
- I declare fat is leaving my body.
- My appetite is curbed through the Holy Spirit and I am satisfied.
- I claim I look and feel good.
- I proclaim I am at my ideal weight.
- I walk briskly without getting out of breath.

My desires are...

_____

_____

_____

_____

_____

_____

50
Guilt and Shame

Have you experienced self-loathing from time to time? All of us go through a feeling of guilt and shame as we remember our past failures. This keeps us from being confident as guilt turns into shame, if not dealt with directly. Guilt is the realization of what you have done and shame is focusing on being a failure and unworthy. These thoughts become very destructive, and wear us down spiritually.

Shame impairs our ability to communicate properly with people especially in times of conflict. Shame leads us to being an introvert removing ourselves from social events. We learn to put these thoughts out of our minds so we may experience the goodness of our Creator. Jesus laid his body for us and took away all our sins and shame so we may be forgiven; thence, we should be quick to forgive ourselves.

Scripture:

*If we confess our sins, he is faithful and just
and will forgive us our sins and purify us from all unrighteousness.*

1 John 1:9 (NIV)

*For the Lord Yahweh will help me. Therefore, I have not been
confounded. Therefore, I have set my face like a flint,
and I know that I shall not be disappointed.*

Isaiah 50:7 (WEB)

Let me not be disappointed, Yahweh, for I have called on you. Let the wicked be disappointed. Let them be silent in Sheol.

Psalm 31:17 (WEB)

He will again have compassion on us; he will tread our iniquities underfoot. You will cast all our sins into the depths of the sea.

Micah 7:19 (ESV)

Fixing our eyes on Jesus, the author and perfecter of faith, who for the joy set before Him endured the cross, despising the shame, and has sat down at the right hand of the throne of God.

Hebrews 12:2 (NASB)

Experiences:

There are many times when we do not listen to the truth and are quick to blame others. We practice getting away from the blaming and shaming and have a more forgiving heart. One type of blaming and shaming occurs with accountability in education when scores are low. Blaming and shaming fosters an atmosphere of distrust and a feeling of being inadequate, which is devastating to a teacher. This is the time we realize the whole community is responsible for educating students, as teachers cannot do it alone.

Another incident was when a substitute teacher had some money stolen from her purse that was open sitting on the teacher's desk. While taking the class to lunch someone took her wallet. Not finding the offender, the substitute demanded her money restored to her. This immediate attention brought on an investigation requiring a review of the camera footage. This created much gossip of blaming and shaming among the teachers.

The wallet and money were never found. However, this was a good learning experience for all the staff members. Being quick to judge and lay blame and shame on a person when we did not witness the act is not ok. When an incident like this occurs, do not get involved or gossip for you did not see it happen.

Confirmations:

- I am confident and fix my eyes on God.
- I am responsible for my actions.
- I am slow to blame and quick to forgive.
- I am accountable for my work.
- I am forgiven of all wrongdoing.
- I am not ashamed or blame others.

Envision and Express the Following:

- I envision myself with a forgiving heart.
- I see myself building up others without condemnation.
- I visualize my path being clear.
- I catch myself listening to the truth before reacting.
- I view myself judging other people fairly.
- I imagine good things about other people.
- My thoughts are pure and my actions are just.
- I let go of past failures.
- I forgive others then move on.
- I fix my eyes upon Christ, the author of perfection.

My desires are...

_____

_____

_____

_____

_____

_____

51
Zeal and Happiness

Happiness can be achieved in every circumstance of life. Zeal is enthusiasm and keeps us going despite our trials. How do we find happiness? We have the power to find happiness through our own determination and energy, choosing to release our negative thoughts.

What affects our happiness most is our attitude with other people in our lives. Be aware that making everyone happy is not a possibility and some people are never happy no matter what is said or done for them. Make the choice to be satisfied in the present celebrating the little things that take place in the classroom. Creating memorable moments with your students include singing, joking, laughing, taking a break to stretch, celebrating birthdays, and holidays.

How can we attain zeal and happiness? We delight in our work serving others and enjoy the present moment. Another way of attaining zeal is going to your happy place. For example, a happy place could be sitting next to a quiet trickling stream or strolling on a white sandy beach, wherever your imagination takes you. We also experience peace through journal writing and reading uplifting spiritual books. Happiness means different things to different people, but in our line of work, it is important to keep a good attitude and find joy in our students and in our accomplishments. We are making a difference molding and shaping the future.

Scripture:

*Not that I speak from want, for I have learned to be content
in whatever circumstances I am. I know how to get along with*

humble means, and I also know how to live in prosperity; in any and every circumstance I have learned the secret of being filled and going hungry, both of having abundance and suffering need.

Philippians 4:11-12 (NASB)

A joyful heart makes a cheerful face, but when the heart is sad, the spirit is broken.

Proverbs 15:13 (NASB)

Make sure that your character is free from the love of money, being content with what you have; for He himself has said, "I will never desert you, nor will I ever forsake you."

Hebrews 13:5 (NASB)

I know that there is nothing better for people than to be happy and to do good while they live.

Ecclesiastes 3:12 (NIV)

Experiences:

As office space was limited, two new special education teachers were placed together in a broom closet. The closet was newly painted and carpeted. The door was left open, for there were no windows or ventilation. Even the students laughed as they passed, knowing it was a broom closet. As difficult as it was, the teachers chose to laugh about it and went about doing their work. Looking back, both teachers were grateful they had a job and it did not matter where they were placed.

Another moment of happiness occurred when after years of intense interventions, our learning-disabled students were dismissed from the special education program. These students met the criteria and closed the educational gap. The parents were delighted with their child's success and the students were proud of themselves for working hard to meet the goals and perform within the grade level. With the parents, we celebrated the joy and happiness of our student's success.

Confirmations:

- I am content with whatever circumstance I am in currently.
- I am productive and resilient.
- I am thankful and grateful for my work and my surroundings.
- I am moving forward to greater things.
- I am happy with what I have now.

Envision and Express the Following:

- I envision myself in a bigger office or classroom.
- I see myself happy and content.
- I catch myself laughing through difficult times.
- I view my students happy and ready to learn.
- I see myself getting better.
- I choose to be comfortable under present circumstances.
- I see humor in every situation.
- I have a smile on my face and a spring in my step.
- I have confidence in my work and myself.

My desires are...

_____

_____

_____

_____

_____

_____

52
Never Give Up

When we are presented with difficult times, it seems everything comes at us all at once. We are tempted to give up and walk away, thinking it will never resolve itself. However, giving up is not the best solution. We overcome obstacles in our path believing that hope does not leave us and through the Holy Spirit, we are showered with love. This is the time to strengthen our faith and trust.

What can you do when feeling down? Call a friend and meet for lunch for some fellowship. In addition, stay in the word by reading scripture to boost your mood by rekindling your mind to a positive and hopeful state. Rejoice always and pray continually in all circumstances. Do you feel like giving up? Never give up, keep persevering, and do not let fear creep into your being. Nothing is impossible with God. Cast your cares and He will sustain you.

Scripture:

But you be strong, and don't let your hands be slack:
or your work shall be rewarded.

2 Chronicles 15:7 (WEB)

Again, therefore, Jesus spoke to them, saying, "I am the light of the
world. He who follows me shall not walk in darkness,
but will have the light of life.

John 8:12 (WEB)

*Rejoice always, pray without ceasing, give thanks in all
circumstances; for this is the will of God in Christ Jesus for you.*

1 Thessalonians 5:16-18 (ESV)

*But Jesus looked at them and said, "With man this is impossible,
but with God all things are possible.*

Matthew 19:26 (ESV)

*For I am the Lord your God who takes hold of your right hand
and says to you, Do not fear; I will help you.*

Isaiah 41:13 (NIV)

Experiences:

Every year we knew teachers who wanted to give up and quit, especially first-year teachers. Some teachers became frustrated with the workload and the profession, but as disheartened as they were, they had to make an adjustment to deal with the stress and fear. Some took sabbaticals or medical leaves for a year to get back on track. Most did return to teaching but had a different attitude upon returning back to school. However, some never returned, finding other careers more to their liking.

Returning teachers shared with us they went to their prayer closet to focus and reflect by reaffirming their faith and aligning with the Spirit. They asked for guidance from the Lord and were given strength and wisdom, for no one grows spiritually without hurdles along the way. Affirmed by renewed faith, teachers went on to finish their careers in education with success.

However, barriers can block our path and keep us from our destiny. Are you feeling stuck? These barriers are not necessarily negative, but used as tools to sharpen our rough edges, refine our character, and polish our silver. Nevertheless, all of us have experienced blocks in our road to success. What God begins He will finish, if we have faith in Him. Psalm 55:22 (NASB) says, "Cast your burden upon the Lord and He will sustain you; He will never allow the righteous to be shaken."

Confirmations:

- I am not giving up but I know my Redeemer is refining my rough edges!
- I am flexible and flowing with love.
- I am called according to His purpose.
- I am successful in whatever I do.
- I am protected by His righteous hand.

Envision and Express the Following:

- I see myself strong with the Lord and give thanks in all circumstances.
- I see my prayers answered.
- I envision myself in a better place with a renewed sense of purpose.
- I see myself with enthusiasm again.
- I catch myself with a good attitude.
- God's hand is with me, guiding me and keeping me safe.
- I do not give up and I turn my darkness to the light!
- I do not grow weary and I prosper.
- I have hope for a good future.
- Nothing is too hard for me; I am making it!
- I have a wonderful and satisfying job.

My desires are...

_____

_____

_____

_____

_____

53
Struggle

We all go through making poor choices that lead us to hurt and pain, bringing strife to ourselves. What kind of choices are you making? Poor choices build on each other, repeating the struggling cycle when we do not seek the Holy Spirit with decisions in our life. We often question our own faith and doubt the comfort when we are going through life's trials pressured by our culture and society.

We lean on our own understanding instead of listening and seeking wisdom. Thereupon, God is power and gives us a way to overcome difficulties if we stay in prayer and close to Him throughout the day. Instead of getting overwhelmed, halt, take a deep breath; take it one step at a time. Then we can rise above and experience victory during our struggles.

Scripture:

We will not boast about things done outside our area of authority.
We will boast only about what has happened within the boundaries
of the work God has given us, which includes our working with you.

2 Corinthians 10:13 (NLT)

Count it all joy, my brothers, when you meet trials of various kinds.

James 1:2 (ESV)

Not only that, we rejoice in our sufferings, knowing that suffering
produces endurance, and endurance produces character,

and character produces hope, and hope does not put us to shame,
because God's love has been poured into our hearts
through the Holy Spirit who has been given to us.

Romans 5:3-5 (ESV)

Do nothing from selfish ambition or conceit, but in humility count
others more significant than yourselves. Let each of you look not
only to his own interests, but also to the interests of others.

Philippians 2:3-4 (ESV)

Now faith is the assurance of things hoped for,
the conviction of things not seen.

Hebrews 11:1 (ESV)

Experiences:

In education, every day can be a struggle and teachers are under tremendous pressure to maintain children's safety and comfort in addition to educating them. This is compounded by students bringing their own baggage to school, leaving the teacher to deal with unexpected behavior and emotions. This can affect the nature of the whole classroom.

There was a student when presented with an assignment, would stare straight ahead, look through us, and stay silent. This child's erratic behavior and refusal to complete work was being defiant and uncooperative. This continued the rest of the year until we started a technology assignment and the youngster became somewhat motivated by the program. The student constantly complained about other children being mean. Despite support, it was difficult to work with this individual because they demanded so much attention.

In such matters, a teacher can be in a great predicament, especially when there is a high student-teacher ratio. Add to the mix a few students with strong personalities having behavioral/emotional issues and you have a big struggle with classroom management. Nevertheless, the teacher is ultimately held responsible and liable to the students' safety, fueling the progression of feeling helpless, hopeless and burned out.

Confirmations:
- I am in the power of Christ when presented with struggles.
- I am making wise choices during calamity.
- I am not forsaken or struck down as God is with me.
- I am strong and courageous, for the Almighty is with me wherever I go.
- I am not frightened or dismayed for when I am weak; I become strong through the Holy Spirit.

Envision and Express the Following:
- I envision myself becoming stronger in spirit.
- I see myself building up more endurance as I work with struggling students.
- I see myself doing nothing from rivalry or conceit, but in humility.
- I visualize myself looking not only to my own interests, but also to the interests of others.
- I see myself in faith, not of men but in the power of God.
- I pray my struggles will not destroy my faith but will instead strengthen it.
- My struggles build up my character and produces endurance and hope.
- I can handle strife through my faith, for He will never leave me or forsake me.
- I pray that God is with me, helping me to think on my feet and be proactive.
- I sing praises to my Lord while I have my being.

My desires are...

_____

_____

_____

54
Fun and Celebration

Being joyous, happy and having fun is a good and perfect gift. We have this time with friends and family to renew our spirit and grow in our faith. As we plan our gatherings, we remember to thank God for bringing these people together for a celebration of life, whatever the occasion.

How do we conduct ourselves at school events? We respect the people who are hosting the events without criticism or complaint. Being with colleagues and having adult conversations away from the classroom has a positive effect on our attitude. We attend these events with a joyous, grateful heart, positive attitude, and good intentions with unconditional expectations.

Scripture:

Also that every man should eat and drink,
and enjoy good of all his labor, is the gift of God.
Ecclesiastes 3:13 (WEB)

Whether therefore you eat, or drink, or whatever you do,
do all to the glory of God.
1 Corinthians 10:31 (WEB)

These things I have spoken to you, that my joy may be in you,
and that your joy may be full.
John 15:11 (ESV)

Let us therefore celebrate the festival, not with the old leaven,
the leaven of malice and evil, but with the unleavened bread
of sincerity and truth.

1 Corinthians 5:8 (ESV)

Experiences:

We had many gatherings for baby and wedding showers, holidays, retirements, and a celebration for high achieving school. Our school had Friday Goodies every other week and the teachers took turns hosting the breakfast with a variety of treats. It set the tone for the rest of the day and the work we had to do.

We also had Fun Friday after school once a month at a location off campus to relax, release stress, and enjoy the end of the week and each other. This brought the faculty together in celebration of our hard work. It lightened our spirit with good conversation, laughter, and fun. On Professional Days, we had activities in the gym just for the faculty and played games before we started our day for team building. We also performed as a faculty for our students at the Talent Show at the end of the school year. The students loved to see their teachers perform as a group having fun. The fun and celebration brought our faculty closer together with joy and sincerity.

Confirmations:

- I am joyous, content, and ready to celebrate.
- I am a fun-loving person.
- I am ready to laugh and enjoy the gathering.
- I am vibrantly alive!
- I am thankful for the opportunity to celebrate with colleagues.

Envision and Express the following:

- I see myself participating in the activities provided.
- I view myself smiling, laughing, and having a good time.
- I perceive myself with a good attitude, sincerity, and truth.
- I see myself in peace with my friends.

- I envision myself socializing with my colleagues and enjoying their company.
- I celebrate who I am.
- I celebrate with my colleagues and their joyous occasions.
- I praise God for my talents.
- I celebrate with good intentions without malice.
- I celebrate other people and their joy.

My desires are...

_____

_____

_____

_____

_____

_____

55
Art and Music

How important are the arts for students? Art and music are important subjects and help students enrich their lives. The arts are fun, relaxing, relieve stress, and help children to better cope with anxiety. It develops language and the left side of the brain. Kids improve coordination and help them stay focused.

The arts contribute to children's emotional and intellectual development, helping with high achievement scores and discipline. Music and art help prepare children for future jobs. Through participation in the arts, students think more creatively, expand their imagination, help with self-confidence and pride of work.

Scripture:

Let the message of Christ dwell among you richly as you teach and admonish one another with all wisdom through psalms, hymns, and songs from the Spirit, singing to God with gratitude in your hearts.
Colossians 3:16 (NIV)

I will sing to the Lord as long as I live; I will sing praise to my God while I have my being.
Psalm 104:33 (ESV)

The trumpeters and musicians joined in unison to give praise and thanks to the Lord. Accompanied by trumpets, cymbals and

*other instruments, the singers raised their voices in praise to the
Lord and sang: "He is good; his love endures forever."
Then the temple of the Lord was filled with the cloud.*

2 Chronicles 5:13 (NIV)

*My lips will shout for joy when I sing praise to you—
I whom you have delivered.*

Psalm 71:23 (NIV)

Experiences:

In times of a budget crunch, we always had to fight to save the arts
in our school. Can the arts improve academic achievement? The arts do
have a big impact on student achievement. They help struggling students
flourish that are often overlooked. The arts are universal and help the
English Language Learners to more fully express themselves.

We had a pupil with difficulty reading and writing because English
was the second language. When he became involved in music and art his
behavior changed, and he developed an exuberant passion of creativity
in both subjects. An exhibition of the student's art at the Convention
Center resulted in a celebration of his achievement with family and the
teachers. Consequently, we saw his self-esteem increase and language
skills enriched through peer conversations. His popularity with other
classmates became apparent through creativity and a fine sense of humor.
Throughout the year, we also saw him develop his writing skills through
these rich experiences. Today he is a successful student in high school
with plans to attend college majoring in the arts.

Confirmations:

* I am in tune with my students.
* I am in the rhythm of life.
* I am open to creativity of the arts.
* I am in song and dance of celebrating my students' passions.
* I am singing praises of my students' achievements.
* I am with the beat of creativity.

Envision and Express the Following:

- I see my students excelling in the arts.
- I see my student's creativity reflected in academics.
- I catch myself looking for ways to enhance my students' lives through the arts.
- I view myself happy taking in the positive energy that is in my students.
- I envision my students' talents valued in God's Kingdom.
- I lift my hands of thanksgiving unto You, Lord.
- My lips sing praises for your goodness in my life.
- My instruments are in tune to worship You, Lord.
- Your love endures forever in my heart.
- The angels of heaven are in unison, chords of faith.

My desires are...

_____

_____

_____

_____

_____

_____

56
Graduation

Graduation is a time to celebrate accomplishments and look forward to a successful future. It is a great milestone and time of joy and happiness. Our students of all ages are graduating and celebrating their hard work. As teachers, we are proud of our children and wish them the best as they go forward with their lives.

How can we measure the dedication and hard work of our students? Our dedication and hard work shows in the sparkle of our students' eyes as they receive their diplomas. May our students be strengthened with all power, endurance, patience, and joy. Rejoice in the Lord and His work in you, to have given you the knowledge to uplift your students to the success of graduation.

Scripture:

I will praise the Lord, who counsels me; even at night my heart instructs me. I keep my eyes always on the Lord. With him at my right hand, I will not be shaken. Therefore, my heart is glad and my tongue rejoices; my body also will rest secure, because you will not abandon me to the realm of the dead, nor will you let your faithful one see decay. You make known to me the path of life; you will fill me with joy in your presence, with eternal pleasures at your hand.

Psalm 16:7-11 (NIV)

Whatever you do, work heartily, as for the Lord and not for men.

Colossians 3:23 (ESV)

The Lord bless you and keep you; the Lord make his face to shine upon you and be gracious to you; the Lord turn lift up his countenance upon you and give you peace.

Numbers 6:24-26 (ESV)

He has shown you, O man, what is good. What does the Yahweh require of you, but to act justly, to love mercy, and to walk humbly with your God?

Micah 6:8 (WEB)

Experiences:

One year, a first grader was physically sensitive to touch. When touched or pushed accidently, the student would turn around and hit other students. It was shared with the parents that their child should be assessed having suspected the need for professional guidance. The mother received the suggestion with high hopes that her child would benefit from receiving additional intervention to improve the academics and physical responses.

Years later, a phone call was received from the mother when this student was graduating from high school. She shared that a written report was required to graduate. In this report, was an explanation of how the help was integral to the success of graduating from high school. The student learned to use strategies to achieve goals. The mother also shared that her child was grateful and many thanks expressed for kindness and compassion for the teacher who cared. The teacher felt happy to see her influence made a difference in this student's success. She attended the celebration and felt very proud.

Confirmations:
- I am completing my tasks as a teacher and the doors are open to me for greater accomplishments.
- I am faithful in God's strength, and I celebrate with thanksgiving.
- I am thankful the Lord has given me wisdom and guidance as I pursue my teaching career.

- I am grateful for being able to influence young minds.
- I am enriched my students are succeeding.

Envision and Express the Following:

- I envision my students' heads decorated with graceful garlands and graduation pendants for their necks.
- I see my students' walking across the stage in their caps and gowns with a diploma in their hands.
- I see my students smiling with joy and excited about their future.
- I view myself moving forward to the next group of students.
- I see myself celebrating and resting.
- My strength is renewed, and I am not weary.
- My heart soars with joy and happiness.
- Well done, my good and faithful servant!
- I reflect on my accomplishments and success.
- The possibilities of the future hold happiness and success.

My desires are...

_____

_____

_____

_____

_____

_____

57

Retirement

How prepared are you for retirement? Retirement is a huge commitment and it is not an easy decision, therefore start preparing early in your career. There are many choices and things to think about when it comes to retirement. When settling to retire, put Christ first in your decision-making plan so He can encourage and help you. This was true for us because through the asking, the answer came that we would retire in two years. This filled our hearts with joy, for we knew it was the right time with the revelation of other plans for our future.

The work force does not necessarily acknowledge nor value the wisdom and experience that comes with age. As hurtful as this is, God knows the time and service we have contributed to His people. Be assured our reward will come as this is registered in the book of heaven. Take time to pray and listen to what is revealed to you. When you open the door to prayer, the answer comes in due time. In addition to your fun and leisure time, include plans for serving God to expand and better His kingdom.

Scripture:

Even to old age, I am he, and even to gray hairs I will carry you.
I have made, and I will bear. Yes, I will carry, and will deliver.

Isaiah 46:4 (WEB)

I have fought the good fight, I have finished the race,
I have kept the faith.

2 Timothy 4:7 (NIV)

*For God is not unjust so as to overlook your work and the love that
you have shown for his name in serving the saints, as you still do.*
Hebrews 6:10 (ESV)

Gray hair is a crown of glory; it is gained in a righteous life.
Proverbs 16:31 (ESV)

Experiences:

Retirement for us was bitter sweet as we both had formidable jobs
that required taxing immediate attention. Leaving on top with distinc-
tion left us happy exiting the school community in good standing. We
had to buy several years so we could afford to live comfortably on our
pension. We met with a financial planner who advised us on all the forms
to complete and deadlines to meet, along with information about Social
Security and Medicare.

As we approached our retirement years, we had lunch together and
contemplated what to do after retirement. We researched many topics,
and then came to a decision to pray for a revelation to unfold. While
meditating, we heard a clear small whisper as God's assignment, to write
an uplifting book for teachers with scriptures to back it up.

We then agreed upon the concept of writing a book and started brain-
storming about the format. The more we researched the more it became
clear that this is the right thing to do to support teachers and advance our
society. We had no doubt how to move forward, and it became effortless.
Teaching is such an intense profession, and so many times we wished for
an inspirational book to support our quest while we were teaching. We
continue to lead an active, productive life for the kingdom of God.

Confirmations:

- I am making wise decisions with the help of the Holy One.
- I am filled with praise and His splendor daily.
- I am still declaring the Lord's awesome deeds.
- I am strong and able to pursue His plan.
- I am using opportunities to further serve God's Kingdom.

Envision and Express the Following:

- I envision myself filled with the Holy Spirit and continuing His work.

- I visualize myself provided for and taken care of now and forever.

- I see myself witnessing and testifying to the faithfulness of God.

- I view myself healthy and enjoying life at my leisure.

- I see myself traveling and having fun with friends.

- Gray hair is a crown of my glory.

- My time and energy make a difference.

- I have an assignment to complete.

- I experience a long, healthy and prosperous life.

- I live an abundant life in retirement.

- I leave an inheritance to my children's children.

- I leave a legacy to my students and the school community.

- My retirement days are better and more productive than my past.

- My retirement days are not the end but just the beginning.

My desires are...

_____

_____

_____

_____

_____

_____

Exercises and Tools to Calm Yourself and Achieve Balance

These are exercises we have learned over the years that have worked for us. We need to take a minute or two at lunch, planning time, or break time to be silent and align ourselves with the Holy Father. The following are a few ways you can relax and align your body. Choose the ones you like best and perform them as needed.

As you are standing, take a deep breath, hold it for a few seconds, and exhale slowly. Repeat this several times.

Stand in a Superman Position in front of your audience to take command of the group. This is a position of power and commanding attention.

Stand and clap around in a circle, crossing the center of your body.

Sit up straight in a chair, take a deep breath and let go, cross your feet then crisscross your arms and hug yourself.

Calm yourself by counting backwards slowly from ten to zero.

Take a deep sigh and let it out to release tension.

Sit in a chair, then cross your ankles. Clasp your hands together and bring them up under your chin. Hold this pose for a few seconds.

Hold onto the back of a chair; jump up and down in place ten times.

Roll your shoulders forward then backward. Repeat several times.

Put your hand over your heart and vocalize your name out loud. Then say something kind about yourself. This is very powerful in building yourself up. For example; "Mary, you are a beautiful and talented person!"

Close your classroom door, turn off the lights, close your eyes, and rest your mind.

Turn off the lights, play soft soothing music to rest and calm your soul.

Always sit up straight and walk with arms and hands slightly turned open. This puts you in a shoulder-back position and gives you more confidence.

Another technique to condition your mind and thoughts to be in the now is to use anchor words. Anchor words act as triggers that are associated with good feelings that bring you back to the present moment. These words can be as simple as Jesus, help, peace, quiet, or silence. These anchor words can be very personal and chosen with care according to your needs or situation.

Take Time to Take Action!

Now is the time to pause and take action to implement these helpful exercises and tools in your life! These will encourage and uplift your Spirit throughout your teaching day. Trust, this makes a big difference for it will keep you balanced and operating in God's light!

Quick Reference Guide of Topics and Scripture

1. **Become Your Dream**
   - Habakkuk 2:2
   - Numbers 12:6
   - Psalm 138:8
   - Genesis 37:9

2. **Stewardship**
   - Matthew 25:21
   - Romans 14:12
   - Proverbs 16:3
   - 1 Corinthians 4:1-2
   - 1 Peter 4:10

3. **Faith and Worship**
   - Hebrews 11:1
   - Matthew 21:22
   - Luke 1:37
   - 1 Corinthians 2:5
   - Matthew 8:26

4. **Values**
   - Luke 6:31
   - Proverbs 16:16
   - Hebrews 13:18
   - Proverbs 10:9
   - James 3:13-14

5. **Gratitude**
   - 1 Chronicles 16:34
   - Psalm 139:14
   - Isaiah 25:1
   - Romans 6:17-18

6. **Obedience**
   - Galatians 5:13-14
   - Colossians 3:22
   - 2 John 1:6
   - Exodus 19:5

7. **Receiving**
   - James 1:17
   - 1 John 5:14-15
   - Matthew 7:11
   - Psalm 112:1-3

8. **Communication**
   - Psalm 141:3
   - Proverbs 18:13
   - James 1:19-20
   - Matthew 12:37
   - Proverbs 15:1-2

9. **Critical Spirit**
   - Matthew 7:1-2
   - 1 Thessalonians 5:11
   - 1 Corinthians 13:7
   - 1 Peter 4:8

10. **Patience**
    - Romans 8:25-26
    - Micah 7:7
    - Isaiah 30:18

11. **Respect**
    - Romans 13:1-2
    - Hebrews 13:17
    - 1 Timothy 5:1-2
    - Titus 2:7-8

12. **Love**
    - 1 Corinthians 13:4-8
    - John 13:34-35
    - Romans 8:37-39
    - Romans 13:8

13. **Change**
    - Joshua 1:9
    - 1 John 2:17
    - Ephesians 4:1-3
    - Ecclesiastes 3:1

14. **Planning**
    - Proverbs 16:3
    - Isaiah 28:29
    - Proverbs 16:9
    - John 14:27

15. **Pride**
    - Philippians 2:3
    - Proverbs 16:18
    - Proverbs 11:2
    - Romans 12:3

16. **Self-Control**
    - 2 Peter 1:5-7
    - 2 Timothy 1:7
    - 1 Corinthians 9:27
    - Galatians 5:22-23
    - Proverbs 25:28

17. **Stress**
    - Psalm 16:8
    - 1 Corinthians 16:13
    - Isaiah 40:31
    - Luke 21:19
    - Jeremiah 17:7-8

18. **Integrity**
    - Proverbs 10:9
    - Philippians 4:8
    - Psalm 41:11-12
    - 1 Timothy 1:5
    - Titus 1:8

19. **Endurance and Perseverance**
    - Isaiah 40:31
    - Romans 12:2
    - Matthew 24:13
    - Hebrews 10:35

20. **Discipline**

- Proverbs 6:23
- Ephesians 6:4
- Proverbs 29:17
- Hebrews 12:11

21. **Setting Goals**

- 2 Chronicles 15:7
- Proverbs 3:5-6
- 1 John 4:18
- Psalm 20:4

22. **Observation and Evaluation**

- Proverbs 9:9
- Proverbs 1:5
- Proverbs 18:15
- Titus 3:14

23. **Manipulation**

- 2 Timothy 3:1-5
- Matthew 7:15
- Romans 16:18
- 2 Corinthians 11:14
- Matthew 24:4

24. **Power of Words**

- Psalm 119:105
- Ephesians 4:29
- 1 Peter 3:10-11
- Proverbs 10:19
- John 1:1

25. **Blessings and Grace**
    - Romans 3:22-24
    - Ephesians 4:7
    - Ephesians 2:8-9
    - 2 Peter 1:2

26. **Humility**
    - Matthew 18:3-4
    - 1 Peter 5:5-6
    - Micah 6:8
    - Proverbs 16:19

27. **Restoration**
    - 2 Corinthians 13:11
    - Galatians 6:1
    - Psalm 51:12
    - Acts 3:20-21

28. **God's Promises**
    - Deuteronomy 31:6
    - Romans 8:28
    - 1 Peter 5:7
    - Isaiah 41:10

29. **Abundance**
    - James 4:2
    - John 14:13-14
    - Mark 11:24
    - Galatians 6:7
    - 1 Timothy 1:14

30. **Temptation**
    - Ephesians 6:10-12
    - Matthew 6:13
    - Romans 12:2

31. **Forgiveness**
    - Mark 11:25
    - Colossians 1:13
    - Hebrews 10:17
    - 1 John 1:9

32. **Fruitfulness**
    - Deuteronomy 7:13
    - Psalm 128:3
    - Psalm 105:24
    - Zechariah 8:12

33. **Kindness**
    - Colossians 3:12
    - Genesis 21:23
    - 2 Samuel 2:6
    - Psalm 117:1-2

34. **Grieving**
    - Psalm 18:28
    - Joshua 1:9
    - Psalm 73:26
    - Matthew 5:4

35. **Healing**
    - Proverbs 17:22
    - Proverbs 4:20-22
    - Isaiah 41:10
    - Acts 9:34

36. **Marriage**
- Proverbs 18:22
- Proverbs 31:10
- Ephesians 4:2-3
- 1 Corinthians 13:4

37. **Living Favor Minded**
- Jeremiah 33:3
- Hebrews 4:16
- Ephesians 1:3
- Timothy 1:14

38. **Compassion**
- 2 Corinthians 1:3-4
- 1 Peter 3:8
- Matthew 5:9
- 1 Peter 4:10
- Psalm 112:4

39. **Making A Difference**
- Galatians 6:9
- Matthew 5:16
- Philippians 1:6
- 1 Corinthians 3:9

40. **Gossip and Lies**
- Ephesians 4:29
- Proverbs 16:28
- Titus 3:2
- Psalm 64:2-4
- Leviticus 19:16

41. Fear and Anxiety

- Deuteronomy 31:6
- Isaiah 41:10
- Psalm 56:3-4
- Matthew 6:25-26

42. Tolerance

- Romans 16:17
- Ephesians 4:2
- Proverbs 16:24
- John 12:47
- Galatians 3:28

43. Depression

- Deuteronomy 31:8
- Psalm 34:17
- 2 Corinthians 1:3-4
- Romans 12:2

44. Rest and Sleep

- Proverbs 3:24
- Psalm 3:5
- Psalm 4:8
- Jeremiah 31:26

45. Disabilities

- Matthew 18:10
- Leviticus 21:18
- Ephesians 2:4
- Matthew 12:22
- Proverbs 17:5

46. Anger and Bitterness
- Proverbs 30:33
- Ecclesiastes 7:9
- Proverbs 15:18
- Psalm 37:8

47. Peace and Quiet
- Psalm 29:11
- Isaiah 55:12
- Matthew 11:28-30
- John 14:27

48. Freedom
- 2 Timothy 1:7
- John 8:32
- 2 Corinthians 3:17
- Galatians 5:13

49. Diet and Dieting
- 1 Corinthians 6:19-20
- John 6:35
- 1 Corinthians 3:16
- Genesis 1:29
- 1 Corinthians 10:31

50. Guilt and Shame
- 1 John 1:9
- Isaiah 50:7
- Psalm 31:17
- Micah 7:19
- Hebrews 12:2

51. **Zeal and Happiness**
    - Philippians 4:11-12
    - Proverbs 15:13
    - Hebrews 13:5
    - Ecclesiastes 3:12

52. **Never Give Up**
    - 2 Chronicles 15:7
    - John 8:12
    - 1 Thessalonians 5:16-18
    - Matthew 19:26
    - Isaiah 41:13

53. **Struggle**
    - 2 Corinthians 10:13
    - James 1:2
    - Romans 5:3-5
    - Philippians 2:3-4
    - Hebrews 11:1

54. **Fun and Celebration**
    - Ecclesiastes 3:13
    - 1 Corinthians 10:31
    - John 15:11
    - 1 Corinthians 5:8

55. **Art and Music**
    - Colossians 3:16
    - Psalm 104:33
    - 2 Chronicles 5:13
    - Psalm 71:23

56. **Graduation**
- Psalm 16:7-11
- Colossians 3:23
- Numbers 6:24-26
- Micah 6:8

57. **Retirement**
- Isaiah 46:4
- 2 Timothy 4:7
- Hebrews 6:10
- Proverbs 16:31

About the Authors

Claire has a BA in elementary education and a Masters in special education, specializing in learning and emotional disabilities K-12 from University of New Orleans, Louisiana (UNO). She also attended the University of Innsbruck, Austria in education and continued her studies in administration. She has over 30 years of service in public schools teaching regular and special education. Writing conferences and classes contribute to her writing success along with radio interviews. She is an Assyrian-American who grew up in New Orleans after emigrating from Iraq with her parents in 1964. Claire lives in Colorado and has two daughters.

Karen has a BS in elementary education from Northwest Missouri State University and a Masters in information and learning technology from University of Colorado, Denver. Her endorsements include library and technology education K-12. She has 26 years of service as a regular education teacher in the parochial schools and a teacher librarian in the public schools. Karen earned many awards including the Gold Apple

Award for excellence in teaching and Highly Effective School Library Program Award by the Colorado Department of Education. She was born in Missouri, grew up on a dairy farm with two brothers, and currently lives in Colorado with her husband. She has a daughter, a son and four grandchildren.

Visit us at our website: maghtaseppsauthors.com

If this book resonates with you, please spread the word to others that could use these resources to implement in their daily lives.

You can visit and explore our website at maghtaseppsauthors.com for comments and questions, leave your email and receive a free pdf.

Order eBooks and paperback books through our website. Visit our Blog posts for current events, articles of interest, and leave comments about the posts.

Get in touch with us through our website or email to arrange speaking engagements.

Share this book in workshops, trainings, meetings, and group sessions.

"Like" it on Facebook and post comments.

Go to Good Reads and Amazon and write a review.

Pick up a copy as a gift for your colleagues and respected teachers.

 Morgan James makes all of our titles available
through the Library for All Charity Organization.

www.LibraryForAll.org

Printed in the USA
CPSIA information can be obtained
at www.ICGtesting.com
JSHW022331140824
68134JS00019B/1408